G000111921

Anne Bateson is a new author. As a seeker of truth, she feels obliged to share her reality with others. For decades, Anne experienced the most profound and downright bizarre situations and events thrusting her without notice or preparation into the realms of the paranormal. She spent her life immersed in books as a prolific reader, why now swap places? And why this book? Her explanation? She feels compelled to enlighten others. She shares her "reality" in a humorous and light-hearted way. Her humour saved her sanity whilst she navigated her way through frightening and curious events.

Anne Bateson

A TRUE STORY

AUSTIN MACAULEY PUBLISHERS™

LONDON • CAMBRIDGE • NEW YORK • SHARJAH

A CIP catalogue record for this title is available from the British Library.

ISBN 9781528980548 (Paperback)
ISBN.9781398408081 (ePub e-book)

www.austinmacauley.com

First Published 2022
Austin Macauley Publishers Ltd®
1 Canada Square
Canary Wharf
London
E14 5AA

Chapter 1

"You're kidding me!"

"I'm not!"

Although my husband Martin thought I was joking at first, I could see from the sparkle in his eyes that he was just as keen as I was to explore the proposition that had just fallen into our laps.

Our friend Lynne had come to me with the idea of setting up a children's nursery, with Martin and I as landlords.

"They don't have the money for a deposit, or to purchase the house," I explained to Martin. "We can be commercial landlords. It'll make a change, and, in all honesty, we wouldn't have to do that much work. Lynne will run the place, and we just take the rent. Think about it! It's a beautiful house."

Those sparkling Irish eyes were the first thing I'd noticed about Martin when I bumped into him on a night out. For me, it was love at first sight and I knew there and then that I would marry him. Six months later, in April 1994, I did.

11 years of marriage later and the pair of us were poring over the details for West Grove, an imposing 1868 house with yellow stone walls, a well and walled grounds. The basement, previously used as a doctor's surgery, was vast and there was

even a disused coach house that I felt sure had potential for all sorts of uses.

Days later, the owner, Dr Stead, a lovely, retired gentleman who seemed almost as old as the house itself, was showing us around. As we wandered, I had to admit it was a tad more dilapidated than the agent's details showed. But it was a beautiful place nonetheless, with high ceilings, deep skirting boards, original marble fireplaces, bay windows and an array of servant bells still intact in the kitchen (although 'kitchen' is a pretty loose description).

During the years that the basement had been used as a surgery, the community would enter the grounds from the front, using a small gate in the stone wall. They'd walk through the garden to the back of the house and enter from ground level into the basement, descending into a small hallway and five rooms which, to this day, have the surgery numbers displayed on the doors.

We followed in their footsteps and discovered that the largest of the rooms – which sits directly beneath the lounge area – was completely bare except for a large stone slab, on a pillar, also of stone, right in the middle of the room.

The slab – a solid block except for a small hole at one end and grooves inlaid around the edge of the stone – was about six feet in length and four feet wide. I never found out for sure what it was but, as you can imagine, when we showed friends around the property, they always joked that this was the slab where the dead bodies were laid out. Over time, I came to think that maybe this was the case. But all these gruesome thoughts were ahead of us. At the time, we shut the door to the basement and looked at each other.

We had fallen in love with the house and had to have it. That's how our relationship worked: we were a team, and together we could achieve anything!

It was a beautiful sunny day, so we decided to take some pictures before we left, to help us discuss ideas for the work needed to bring this building back to life.

I was usually completely inept with a camera, but I gave it my best shot (pardon the pun) and snapped away. Something suddenly caught my eye. What was that? Did I see a figure at the window? For a fleeting moment, I felt cold. I shook the feeling off and thought I'd look carefully at the photos when they were developed.

The sale went through in just two weeks. Then, like a bolt out of the blue, came the phone call that turned everything on its head.

Lynne had changed her mind.

Of course, she apologised but what were we to do? Was this a sign not to proceed? I like to think I act intuitively but… I wasn't sure.

It was such a beautiful house; I recalled the photo – we still didn't have an explanation for the large grey misty shadow outside the window where I thought I'd seen a figure. The mist was outside an upstairs window, so it couldn't possibly be the camera flash reflection, and the sun wasn't able to cause this.

But we didn't give it that much thought. We were so preoccupied with our plans for the restoration.

We had to go ahead; we couldn't lose the deposit – it was a substantial sum. In the end, we decided that our only option was to rent out our current home and move into West Grove while the renovations were completed. The Irish eyes were still smiling, just about!

The day dawned, we were proud owners of a beautiful, original home (well two homes really), and although we were somewhat daunted by the workload needed to restore the place and having to move from our current home (which had taken us two years to find) we were still excited to restore this beauty.

Chapter 2

It was only a few days before West Grove started showing us more mysterious goings on.

Martin was in the house on his own, preparing for the entourage of contractors due to descend within the next few days. He was on the phone, dealing with a problem, when he heard an almighty bang from upstairs. It was so worryingly loud that he asked the caller to hold and ran upstairs to see what had happened.

Not seeing anything, he thought perhaps a door had slammed shut. But all the doors were open, and everything was quiet.

Martin finished his call and phoned me, somewhat alarmed. He didn't mind admitting that he had been scared. We chatted for several minutes, trying to rationalise what he'd heard. We couldn't fathom it, but as with the 'mist' in the photo, we put it to the back of our minds.

The refurbishment proceeded as planned, although we discovered much later that we could have been killed at any time by the illegal actions of the so-called plumber we'd hired. That, and the ensuing court case proved something that my now dearly departed mother would say regularly: "It's not the dead you need fear – they can't harm you. It's the living you need to worry about!"

Besides, despite the age of the house and the unusual events, we didn't think, at this point, that we were sharing our home with dead people.

We celebrated our housewarming with a lovely couple, friends from Manchester. The celebration was merry and prolonged, and although I was slightly worse for wear, my friend and I didn't have a care in the world, as the two of us danced to our favourite tracks in the lounge.

Suddenly, a large, grey mist shape appeared out of nowhere. Roughly the size of a small sofa, it appeared in the middle of the room and moved as one whole mass across the room and passed through the wall.

My face must have been a picture. I didn't necessarily sober up, but it was a sobering thought, albeit one that I kept to myself. I can still recall the incident as though it was only yesterday; it's so etched on my mind. I didn't tell Martin – I knew he would say I was drunk and imagining it.

I reflected on this vision for many months because I simply couldn't explain to myself what it was. But again, the memory faded, as did the hangover (thankfully) and daily life went on.

Shortly after that incident, Martin and were in the kitchen, enjoying a coffee. We rarely found time to do that, and it was lovely to just sit and chat quietly.

But our peace was shattered by a very loud repeated knocking at the front door. We jumped out of our skins and froze mid-conversation.

You see, no-one ever came to that door. To do so, they'd have to enter through a gate that doesn't open, which is some distance from the house. Then, they'd have to walk across the expanse of garden, where there isn't even a path. So, we'd never heard a knock at that door, let alone anyone rapping the knocker as loud and repeatedly as this.

The style of the house is typical for its age, with front and back entrances in the middle. The rooms are either side, and all accessed from the central hall.

We both peered nervously out of the bay window of the dining room, to see who could be knocking so insistently. But despite a good view of the garden, we couldn't see a soul.

We quickly left the dining room, darting across the hall to the lounge, which had another large bay window with a good view of the surrounding garden. Again, no-one was around. It was baffling. There was no way in or out of the walled garden.

As we finished our coffee in the kitchen, we pondered the mystery.

It was all a bit strange – but the puzzle deepened even more a few days later. Call me strange, but my form of meditation is to do housework. I was busy cleaning when realisation struck.

I opened the front door, and just as I thought, there wasn't a knocker! It sounds insignificant but at the time, it didn't feel it. We've never been able to explain the mystery of the knocker, knocking without a knocker!

Around this time, I began to form my own rationale. I believe – you might not agree – in residual energy. I think the knocking was a type of memory from the distant past when visitors would knock on the door.

Chapter 3

With the finishing touches now being added to the house, any worries we'd had about continuing with the purchase had vanished.

This was our home. We'd displayed our framed photos in the hall, organised our books, put up our pictures and found places for our ornaments.

The photos weren't regular family stuff, though. Martin and I were amateur boxing coaches and most of the framed pictures related to our work in the gym we'd set up in 1996. His background as a boxer and mine as a ballet dancer and fencing champion seemed to naturally lead us into coaching roles. I'll tell you more about our exciting success later.

One photo was a group shot of four of our young boxers, all of whom had won significant amateur boxing titles. It wasn't in a special place or a special frame – it just sat among the others on the radiator cover – but over a couple of years, we'd regularly hear an awful racket and find just that photo face down in the centre of the hall, as if it had been thrown there.

It was the only one that suffered such activity. We tried moving things round and putting it where the other photos were displayed but it made no difference. It was always the same frame, face down, in the middle of the floor.

To understand what was happening, we tried causing enough vibration in the area to make the photo move or slide or fall off. But it didn't move. It only happened during the night, when we were asleep – and it would always wake us with a start. Oddly, though, it never broke, even though the floor is made of hardwood.

One night – I remember it vividly because it was a rare occasion when I was home alone overnight – I was woken by an almighty crashing sound. I instantly sat up in bed and listened for noises of anyone moving around. I don't mind admitting I was scared: I could feel and hear my heart thumping in my chest. What should I do? I was too scared to leave the bedroom to check on things but was also too scared to go back to sleep without checking on things, damn it!

Eventually, I plucked up the courage to leave the bedroom. I flicked all the lights on, to make me feel less spooked. Slowly, carefully, I ventured part-way down the stairs – all the while talking to myself to try to reduce the fear! And there it was, that same picture in the middle of the floor, face down.

I crept all the way downstairs and picked it up (why was I creeping?). Sure enough, it wasn't broken. I put it back in its usual place and, although this sounds rather silly now, I said out loud, "If there's anyone here now and you're trying to scare me, it's worked. Please don't do it again. I'm on my own – you know that. And I want to go back to bed and sleep."

I stood for a minute or so and went back up the stairs.

I left the lights on for the rest of the night and thankfully, there were no further interruptions. I was so relieved when Martin returned.

But I digress. Although, there is a conclusion to this little story, although it wasn't revealed until years later.

Chapter 4

Word spread within the sporting community about our boxing gym, and we were soon delivering regular sessions to both amateur and professional sportspeople. The media was showing a keen interest, particularly in the young talent that was developing there.

Things were going very well, and we were meeting wonderfully interesting people. Preoccupied with the business, we were very happy and felt blessed to have such an interesting and fulfilling life. You could say we were following our dreams.

We'd enjoyed a fantastic holiday in Florida and had invited some friends we'd spent time with there to visit for the evening.

We'd only just exchanged pleasantries – we hadn't even moved out of the small entrance area – when out of nowhere we heard loud, prolonged laughter. The closest I can get to describing it is a 'witch's cackle'.

We froze mid-sentence, and stood there, staring at each other. I broke the spell (pardon the pun) by asking to look inside their bag. I fully expected to find a joke gadget, and that they'd fall about laughing, having given me a good scare.

Nope, there was nothing but two bottles of white Zinfandel – a nod to our recent holiday.

I looked outside and said, "Have you brought the children with you? Did you leave them out here, wanting to surprise me?"

Nope again. No kids. I shut the door.

We looked at each other and asked what we'd heard. We all agreed: loud cackles like a prolonged laugh, just as though someone was standing in between us. We had no explanation, and, as the wine flowed, we put it to the back of our minds.

We only meet up rarely now, but even all these years later, we still talk about it, and still find it unexplainable.

There was a lot of activity around doors and entrances. Often, I would be home alone and clearly hear Martin come in. I'd shout hi but when he didn't appear, I'd go to the door to discover he wasn't home.

And it wasn't just me – Martin experienced the same. Even when we were both sitting in the lounge, we'd think we'd heard footsteps in the hall and the door opening and closing as though someone had come in. We often got up and went to look, simply out of curiosity, but there was no-one there.

Our youngest daughter, Aaron, was only 10 years old when we moved into the house. She hadn't yet experienced any of these strange events – and that was how we wanted to keep it. Besides, we didn't dwell on any of the incidents. Life was busy, we were very happy in our relationship and our working lives, so we didn't have time to worry too much. Things happened, but infrequently enough for us to banish them from the conscious mind (if not the subconscious).

But all that was going to change. Other incidents were to follow, and one was to involve our daughter. But more of that later…

Chapter 5

It was a Saturday evening – always a welcome respite, as it was one of the few times the gym was closed. We weren't at a tournament, coaching the boxers, and what's more, our youngest, Aaron, was away on a sleepover.

Instead, Martin and I were enjoying a night to ourselves, sharing a bottle (or two) of red wine. Martin was listening to music on his headphones, while I was watching my favourite TV programme (happily without interruption and bloke comments).

I must admit though, my thoughts were drifting. I started thinking about my dad, who had passed many years previously, when I was relatively young. I was pondering whether he'd be proud of me. Would he be pleased with our achievements? Although thinking about him made me sad, I was happy to conclude that I was sure he would be proud of how I was living my life.

Feeling so relaxed and content, I found it startling when, out of nowhere, a large, white feather came floating down from the ceiling in the middle of the room. When I say large, it was bigger than any feather I'd ever seen, about a foot long.

As I watched the feather fall, I distinctly remember thinking, "Wow! Look at that! It's beautiful and so white."

I recall laying back on the sofa, intensely focused on this feather. On impulse, I placed one hand on the floor and reached out with the other hand to the middle of the room. I extended my arm as far as I could reach and simply waited for the feather to fall into my outstretched hand.

Just before it did, Martin removed his headphones and said, "What are you doing?"

"I'm catching that feather," I replied.

"What feather?"

At that moment, the feather landed on my hand and simply disappeared.

I didn't move for a short while, pondering what had just occurred. I remember Martin shaking his head and laughing gently, more to himself really, obviously wondering what on earth I was thinking.

I pretended to go back to watching my programme, so Martin wouldn't have anything else to say, but I couldn't concentrate on the TV at all.

What had happened? I know what I saw and can still see it clearly to this day. I know I acted instinctively by reaching out for the feather, without rationalising that a feather can't possibly, simply appear in the middle of a room and fall from the ceiling.

But there you have it. It happened. Go figure!

Chapter 6

Some weeks later, it was our turn to host a sleepover for our youngest, Aaron. The house was finally finished, so it was about time she had a friend stay.

As usual, we shopped together for her friend's visit – it was all part of the fun of the evening, buying party food and treats for them to share. If I recall correctly, a midnight feast was on the cards, to be eaten under the blankets by torchlight.

The evening passed quickly, and fun was had, but it was soon time to sleep, or at least attempt to calm the excitement and eventually drift off. Sure enough, by midnight, when I looked in on the girls, they had unknowingly foregone their midnight feast, and tiredness had won. I dimmed the lights, left them sleeping soundly and went to bed myself.

What on earth? We were woken out of a deep slumber by the two girls, who were standing in our bedroom doorway, completely petrified. It took me longer to come round than Martin – he seemed much more coherent.

The girls were crying and saying they'd seen a ghost in their room. Confused, I got out of bed and attempted to comfort them. I asked what had happened.

Although they kept repeating that they had seen a ghost, they were so visibly shaken up that they struggled to get the words out clearly.

When they finally began to calm down, I asked them to explain in a little more detail. I assumed they'd been dreaming or imagining things and I believed I'd be able to rationalise to them what had happened. It was the middle of the night and foremost in my mind was the thought that they needed to go back to bed and get to sleep.

They both began to speak at once, explaining that they had seen a dark grey mist 'standing' at the window. Although it was misty, they could clearly make out the figure of a young girl, dressed in a long, old-fashioned dress. She was looking into the distance, out of the window, with her hands clasped together, and they both stood and took the position of the supposed apparition.

They said they didn't know why they'd woken but when they both opened their eyes and saw the girl, they immediately dived under the bed covers in fear. They had stayed there for a short while, whisperingly discussing the possibility that they'd imagined a shadow and were being silly. They agreed to look again, at the same time.

The girl was still standing there.

It was then that they leapt out of bed and came running across the landing to our bedroom, screaming and crying. I tried to calm them without any real success, so we agreed they could sleep in another bedroom for the rest of the night. Thankfully, there were no more incidents.

I felt terrible for Aaron's friend. When her mother came to collect her, I didn't know whether to tell her but decided, rightly or wrongly, to leave it to the young girl to share the story if she wanted to. I never heard anything further about it from either of them.

But Aaron wouldn't go upstairs on her own at all during the evening and refused to sleep in her room for another six weeks. She slept on the sofa until she was brave enough to return.

I couldn't show any fear at the time but, although the incident was never repeated, if I was alone in the house, I wouldn't look in the direction of her room for a long time afterwards.

Chapter 7

Noises from the main door and hallway had by now become a regular event. We got so blasé about it that we pretty much gave up investigating – although I remember one day being so convinced that Martin had returned with our daughter that I was annoyed when they didn't answer my questions about how their day had been. Of course, I should have known; when I opened the door from the kitchen to the hall, I realised why they hadn't replied – they weren't there!

It was then that I started to register that the strange events were becoming frequent and a tad difficult to ignore. I remember not being particularly scared by this but feeling confusion and curiosity. Was it that residual energy again?

The house renovations finished, we decided to have a party to celebrate with family and friends. Invitations were made, the night arrived, and it was lovely to have everyone together.

Soon, the party was in full swing, and friends were scattered in little groups around the house. They'd given us lots of compliments about what we'd done to the place, which was nice to hear. My mother was having such a great time and, despite getting on in years, was the life and soul of the party. She was dancing with us, and generally reminiscing to the sounds of the 60s and 70s. We were having a blast.

Everyone who knew Mum will remember that she loved taking photos. At the drop of a hat, she'd whip out her camera and start snapping away. Now that she's no longer with us in the physical realm, we all miss having such a prolific photographer around.

This evening was no exception. Mum took lots of photos. But when we eventually saw the images, they didn't take us back to the fun of the evening. In fact, they gave us more cause for concern.

We had no close neighbours, so the music was blaring out. Later in the evening, all three of my daughters, a few girlfriends and I established ourselves upstairs in my bedroom, to have a little time out and be able to hear ourselves speak. Oh – there was one token boy (one of our boxers) with us, enjoying the female company and chat.

Out of the blue, my eldest daughter Dionne said, "It's really weird, but my legs are tingling!"

That stopped us in our tracks. We all stood looking at her, in silence.

"Listen," she said.

We did and oddly, we could all hear her leather knee-length boots creaking for no reason.

I'm not sure how long we stayed silent. It almost felt like time had stopped.

I broke the silence with, "Oh yes, I can hear that! How strange."

All the time, I was thinking something very different. I didn't want to say it out loud and scare anyone, but that tingling sensation really didn't sound weird – it's something that happens often to me, usually when I'm going to sleep. But there's more to that tale, which I will divulge later.

As we all stood, listening to the bizarre creaking of the leather boots, suddenly and without any rational explanation, a pair of bookends (a gift from my youngest, in the shape of two entwined elephants) came hurtling off the chest of drawers and landed about two feet away in the middle of the floor.

If it hadn't been so extraordinary, it would probably have been a hilarious sight.

I stood there thinking, "What the hell just happened?" when someone echoed my thoughts, blurting out, "What the hell just happened?"

We all agreed that the bookends, which had been in the middle of the chest of drawers, not near the edge, had just flown past us. I picked the bookends up and replaced them on the drawers.

"Okay, then", I said to the room, "Whoever has just done that, do it again."

They didn't. Party pooper!

The incident ended our little get-together, and we all decided to make our way back downstairs to re-join the party.

"Great," I thought, "I sleep in there!"

We didn't dwell on what had happened: who has the time for that? But it was mentioned once or twice through the following years when we got together as a family. We still have no explanation for it, nor has it happened again since, but it's an extraordinary family memory.

When we downloaded Mum's photos to my laptop, we were shocked to discover that all those taken in the lounge were full of 'orbs'.

For anyone not familiar with the terminology, orbs are round balls of light, generally thought of as the manifestation of energy. Often they emit their own light, and are thought to be spirits –the energy of people who've passed on.

It was in the lounge that I'd seen the mist shortly after we moved in, when our friends from Manchester came over to celebrate our new home. Then, I'd carried on dancing and not confided my strange experience to anyone but today, everyone could see the orbs in every part of the photos. There were so many, they'd created a kind of mist effect.

I still have the photos saved on the laptop and I still don't have any rational explanation for the strange glowing circles. In fact, previous residents and visitors joining in the fun is probably the most rational idea I can think of.

Chapter 8

In the days after the party, I considered what had happened with a clear head. I thought about everything, the other strange events going on in the house, the orbs in the photos etc. I began to wonder what was happening as it was becoming increasingly hard to ignore it all.

Pondering the events triggered a memory from my childhood. Growing up, it became a bit of a standing joke that if Mum had a dream about either me or my brother, we would ask her not to tell us.

It was because, on more than one occasion, she had dreamt about someone, and the events came true. Nothing major, but one in particular sticks in my mind.

I was about 12 years old, which, believe me, was some considerable time ago. It was before we'd all left for work and school, and Mum was in the kitchen. We were chatting away when she suddenly changed the subject completely and told me she'd had a dream the night before about her friend Jane's son Simon. In the dream, he'd fallen over and cut his knee open and had to be taken to hospital.

Later that day when Mum arrived home, she said: "You know that dream I had? Well, Jane told me today that Simon had fallen in the garden and cut his knee. She'd had to take him to hospital for stitches."

There you go!

This was a regular occurrence with Mum – hence us saying that we didn't want to know if she dreamed about us. We laughed about it, but at some level, it unsettled me.

This leads nicely onto another childhood memory, which is much more bizarre but also completely true. Here goes…

Chapter 9

It was relatively early in the morning, and I was ready for school. Although my brother and I went to different high schools (this was back in the day, when the local schools were separate for girls and boys) we walked together whenever it was appropriate.

We were rushing about as usual, when Mum appeared, in her dressing gown. She saw the confused looks on our faces.

"I'm not feeling well," she told us. "I had a bad night. I had a dream that wasn't pleasant and couldn't get back to sleep, so I'm not going in to work today."

We shrugged it off as just another one of her dreams – but it was a rarity that she didn't go into work.

"It was very strange," she continued, "I dreamt that a man had been knocked off his bike and killed by a petrol tanker."

At the time, we lived in a small village relatively close to a large petro-chemical plant, and until a new spur road was built, heavy volumes of petrol tankers would pass our home.

"It was so real that I woke your father up and told him about it. I had to put my dressing gown on and step outside the front door – even though it was the middle of the night – to see if there was anything or anyone there. Everything was quiet, but it shook me up. It just seemed so real.

"I couldn't get back to sleep, and neither could your father, so I came downstairs and made a pot of tea.

"When I got back to bed, he said, 'I've had a funny dream too. I dreamed that my sister Betty called me, and you'd answered. You called me to the phone, saying that Betty had something important to tell me, but I woke up before I could get there.'"

Mum said they'd discussed his dream for a while, curious about it, especially as he hadn't spoken to his sister in a while.

Dad probably didn't think too much about it during his busy day. As a self-employed painter and decorator, he'd often work on large properties for months on end. At that time, he was working at a pub in the area he grew up in. He'd been chatting to the landlord, who'd mentioned a few of the regulars. One stood out as someone Dad thought he'd been to school with.

Dad liked to have a couple of pints at the weekend so he asked the landlord to mention to the school friend that he was working at the pub and would pop in over at the weekend for a pint with him.

The following day, the landlord confirmed the friend would be in over the weekend and was looking forward to catching up for old times' sake.

As usual, we arrived home from school before Dad got in from work. Mum didn't look much better.

"What's wrong?" I asked.

"Well, it's awful but do you remember my dream?" she said.

I nodded and she continued.

"There was a man knocked off his bike last night by a tanker. He was killed. It was on the news this morning when I was listening to the radio. I can't believe it."

While I felt quite upset about the accident, the fact that Mum had told us about her dream before hearing the news, was also very strange. And it was about to get even stranger.

A while later, my dad arrived home and as soon as he entered the kitchen, he said, "You'll never guess what! The guy I was supposed to be meeting in the pub – the guy who I went to school with – well, he was knocked off his bike last night by a tanker and killed."

The complete and utter silence seemed to last for an age.

I was a little scared by how the events had unfolded. I pushed it to the back of my mind. It was unsettling to think that you could somehow know about things before they'd happened. I felt sad for the man and his family, too. It was a mixture of feelings that upset me for days afterwards and it was difficult to shake off the strange way things had unfolded.

Little did I know that I would, in the future, begin to experience such things myself.

Chapter 10

I was 17 years old when my life changed profoundly.

There I was, working in the city, enjoying a carefree life, and completely unaware and unprepared for this journey to begin.

It started with a dream.

But it was different to the usual dream. I woke with a deep feeling of sadness. In my dream, I'd witnessed a plane crash. It was extremely vivid and felt like I was there, observing events and among the action but not feeling at all stressed or fearful.

The scene changed dramatically to debris floating on the sea and when I focused on a doll among it all, I recall feeling overwhelmed by the sight.

During the dream, I felt deep sadness for the people that hadn't survived.

When I awoke, I knew it was real and not just a terrible nightmare. At the time, I wouldn't have been able to explain how I knew.

But why me? Why did I experience this?

As this journey has unfolded, I believe I've found answers to those questions.

I felt sad for several weeks and often pondered on the dream, re-running the images over and over in my mind. I didn't intentionally want to relive the experience, but it was so intense that it overpowered me for a while.

Some weeks later, there was an article on the TV news about a plane crash into the ocean that had killed everyone on board.

Was this what I had 'seen'?

I couldn't shake the memory of the doll. Clearly it would have belonged to a child, which made the dream even more poignant.

I recall the sense of hopelessness I felt: I'd had an insight into this tragedy before it happened, but why?

I didn't have time to reflect for too long. I was busy working and spending time with friends. I parked the experience for the time being and life went on, although a small measure of sadness remained with me.

A year passed. Memories fade and life dealt me a severe blow; my dad died suddenly of a heart attack. He was 45 and I was 18.

I celebrated my 18th birthday, spending time at the hospital with him and that was the last time I saw him. I was the last person to be with him, and I am forever grateful for that.

Eventually, I emerged from this tragic event and got on with my life, as everyone must.

About a year after Dad's death, I had a second significant dream. Again, I was an observer of unfolding events. This time, I was walking in a building that was collapsing all around me but, as before, I felt completely safe and unworried.

The scene was in full colour and incredibly vivid. One minute, I was in the collapsing building with full sound and visual detail, and the next I was walking outside.

The scene on the street was devastating. Women dressed in black clothing were running around, sobbing, and hysterical. There were children laying on the ground.

I recall walking among these people, but I was unseen by them. Their lives were playing out before me, but they were unaware of me.

Once again, I awoke in tears, consumed with a feeling of overwhelming sadness. I couldn't shake the feeling.

How do I make sense of this? Why has it happened again?

A feeling of dread remained and didn't disperse for several weeks.

And then a news article appeared. A school in Italy had collapsed, resulting in the death of several children. I felt sick. Was that what I saw? But how could I be there – particularly before it happened?

This time I couldn't shake it off. I had to tell someone, but who? I didn't have any rational explanation and I knew I had to move on from this, but I can't overemphasise the feeling that I was emotionally involved. It took a long while for the vivid thoughts to leave my mind.

Around this time, I began to have a problem with my watch. When I wasn't wearing it, it worked perfectly. But when I put it on, the second hand sped up and it gained time.

Wow! How does that happen?

Someone – I can't recall who – told me it can be caused by static electricity.

Well, it was funny they should say that, because I had a problem at work too.

When I walked around the office, the static built up so much around me that I not only got shocks from items of furniture, but the word processor would start typing before my fingers were even placed on the keys! And the photocopier would begin copying when I walked past or into the photocopying room.

My employers paid for the whole floor to be sprayed with some sort of product to reduce the electric charge.

Some years later, I had an epiphany moment. Maybe I'm picking up messages, like a radio or a TV? My rationale is that the signals that become sounds and images are all around us constantly. But we can't see or hear them unless we power up the devices and tune into the right frequency. Maybe the static build-up around me, which was exceptional, was the cause of me tuning in?

Talking of TVs, that was impacted too. My TV at home began turning over regularly, even though I was nowhere near the remote control! Strange but true.

This 'tuning in' led to a third dream. It was even more depressing than the previous two. So much so that I've never told the full story to anyone, out of respect for the victim.

I recall the overwhelming sense of sadness, but I felt helpless too. The questions bubbled up again. Why am I experiencing this? What's the point if I can't do anything about what's going to unfold?

After this third dream, I didn't hear anything on the news or read anything that related to it, so you might ask if it happened. But I feel certain it did. It was another in the series of vivid dreams that I can remember to this day.

It's difficult to explain, but just as with the first dream, I felt sure that it was a tragic event, rather than a dream or nightmare. These dreams were just different. I believe the fact that I vividly recall such events many years later is testament to the fact that they weren't the usual, easily and speedily forgotten, dreams.

It upset me so much that I prayed that I would never experience such devastating dreams ever again. To date, I haven't.

The 'dreams' continued but in a much lighter vein.

Sure enough, the next one was remarkable in a different way – and the events unfolded not weeks later but the very next day.

I dreamt there was a chemical plant explosion. People living nearby were evacuated elsewhere and, just as before, I was walking around the temporary premises but not being seen. Just as if I was watching a movie, I saw them camping out there and although it was only a brief snapshot of a dream, I woke with an instant feeling of relief. People had been inconvenienced but there were no deaths or injuries. That alone brought a smile to my face.

I went to work as usual, delighted not to be worried about an impending tragedy. I told a friend about the dream, happy that it hadn't left me with that feeling of overwhelming sadness.

When I got home, the TV was on, and the evening news started. Not only were they reporting the very same story, but the images shown of the evacuated locals were identical to what I'd seen in my dream.

I stood in shock. How had this happened? The incident and evacuation had happened the previous night – was it while I was dreaming? Was I there? How could I have been there?

It sounds ridiculous but the main thoughts running through my mind were that I'd dreamed the event while it was taking place – and the images shown on TV matched what I'd seen.

Trying to rationalise this latest development, I called the friend I'd spoken to that day and talked it through. Sharing the experience somehow made it easier. I was pleased there wasn't a tragedy but the timing of it took things to another level, and in all honesty, it shook me up.

Years later, I felt forced to find answers to it all, but first I had yet another dream. And it was all quite hilarious.

The vision began with a plane coming in to land over my head, as though I was standing close to the runway. As it neared the ground, the plane tilted to one side but managed to land safely. After the emergency landing, a temporary slide appeared, and the passengers evacuated safely.

Why on earth did I have a vivid dream about that?

In the morning, I shared it with the same friend. I purposely told her as many details as I could. I described the colour of the decals on the plane and told her which side it toppled to. I was excited – it felt like I had a witness.

Later, we were both at our own homes, getting ready for a night out, when she called me.

"Have you got the TV on?" she asked.

"No," I replied.

"Turn it on."

"Why?"

"Just turn it on."

She sounded very excited, so I did as I was told. Again, my very brief dream unfolded exactly as I had described it.

The local news was reporting an emergency landing that had ended safely.

I hadn't any reason to make anything up, but this was proof that I was telling the truth. And it was a relief to know that, finally, someone else knew it was all real.

It was to be several years before I had another dream. It was well worth the wait though and it brought with it a very positive outcome following a devastating tragedy, and a bizarre twist.

But that's to come later.

Chapter 11

When we'd opened our gym, in the mid-1990s, our ethos was to welcome anyone and everyone who wanted to take part. At that time, boxing was a 'closed shop', in the sense that if you weren't interested in boxing competitively, there was no rhyme or reason for you to be in the gym. Most coaches were busy enough with competing boxers to accommodate non-competitive trainees.

As well as that, most boxing gym facilities weren't conducive to public participation – they certainly weren't up to the usual gym standards. We, on the other hand, had men's and women's changing rooms, showers and toilets.

Don't get me wrong, our boxing gym was still a spit and sawdust type of space. It was housed in an old warehouse, with bare brick walls, metal beams and girders: the industrial look worked well.

But our philosophy was 'fitness for all'. Boxing is very much about fitness training, and many people welcomed the opportunity to experience that first-hand, without having to get into the ring and spar.

I remember being surprised that it wasn't just local lads who were keen, but every sector of the community. I particularly wanted to encourage women to get involved, and what better way to do that than becoming a coach and being a positive role model?

Little did I know what that would lead to.

I have lots of stand-out memories from my time coaching boxing alongside my husband, and one of the main ones is the live radio interview I did quite early on in my coaching career at the BBC Radio 5 Live studios.

The presenter, Peter Levy, was off air for a short while as I was escorted into the studio. He greeted me and then said, "I'm going to be controversial; you know."

No pressure then!

But little did he know that I'd had a career in public relations and considerable experience dealing with the press, so I wasn't too fazed. In fact, if I'm honest, I was quite looking forward to the challenge.

The controversy was around women in boxing. It's an old chestnut that really seems even older now that times have changed, but at the time, it was a divisive topic.

Adding to the pressure, England Boxing, then called the Amateur Boxing Association of England, kept the sport strictly regulated and they weren't – to put it politely – particularly keen on women in boxing. So, I suppose I was breaking ground in the ranks of amateur boxing. I didn't feel as though I needed to blaze a trail for women, but that's what was happening by default.

The 20-minute interview just flew by. Peter Levy kindly congratulated me and said that although he'd tried to be controversial, he felt that I'd got the better of him and held my own.

I accepted his praise with a smile. I hoped I'd helped break down barriers and dilute prejudice towards women participating in a male-dominated sport. I did my little bit for the cause and clearly, things have now changed massively in that regard.

My decision to become a boxing coach was proving to be most enjoyable – and it caused quite a stir elsewhere in the media too.

I came to boxing training having been a ballet dancer since the age of four. I got into fencing at high school and became school and county fencing champion. I had my own pony, so rode a lot – and swam a lot too.

I was already very active, and Martin introduced me to boxing training to keep fit. An ex amateur boxer himself, who'd fought more than 70 bouts, he was passionate about the benefits.

My knees are pretty worn out, so I struggled to do anything active that didn't impact my knees, so I thought why not give it a go? Much to my and Martin's surprise, I took to it like a duck to water, and I've not stopped since. But I digress.

I'm not sure how the local press heard about us, but they loved the headline 'Ballet to Boxing' and ran photos and the story. That led to a piece on local TV news. They filmed us training (so far so good), but the film crew thought it a good idea to open with a shot of us walking hand in hand into the gym. We had to do a few takes because we were giggling so much.

Although we appreciated the publicity and recognition, we cringed somewhat at our 15 minutes of fame – and that wasn't the end of it. As time passed, our boxers began to win titles, which created an awful lot of interest – and the local media were regular visitors to the gym.

Then the national press got hold of the story.

I had a bit more cringing to do when I got a call from my brother, who certainly didn't phone often.

"Hi Anne, it's Pete. I've just been reading my newspaper, the Daily Star…"

"You read the Daily Star? It's readable?"

"I get it for the football."

"I believe you, thousands wouldn't."

"Well, I was reading it and I called out to Andrea, 'There's a woman in the paper here who looks just like Anne!' I had a closer look and read the caption and shouted, 'It is Anne!'"

I know. I made the News of the World too. The story of ballet to boxing. Who'd have thought?

Several national newspapers contacted me asking if I would sign a contract for an exclusive, with pictures and an interview. To be honest, I was embarrassed.

There I was, enjoying myself, running a successful venture in Leeds, minding my own business, and I was being pursued for an exclusive!

Once, when my horse was in the wrong field, the farmer called for me to go and sort it out, urgently. This was then followed by another call asking where the farm was, so a journalist could meet me there to conduct an interview. I kid you not. I declined to give the address and thought that was it.

But the pursuit continued.

I agreed to do a double page spread in the Sunday Times. The interview was done over the telephone and included my career history, particularly my time selling tractors around the world.

A photographer was dispatched to shadow me in the gym for a whole day. He asked for several shots, including one of me in a tutu, on my pointes, with boxing gloves on. It's a very difficult pose to hold but I'm a consummate professional, so I persevered – just.

The photographer was a guy called Brendan Monks. I was slightly overwhelmed as he had a very illustrious career as a professional sports photographer and had worked with the best in the world. I recall him saying that our gym was one of the best he'd been in – a compliment indeed.

I still have the shots, although the article didn't appear because, would you believe it, I didn't have any photographs of me selling tractors! But it was a most enjoyable and unique experience and one that I'll never forget.

Chapter 12

They were busy times, as we worked hard to build up the gym. And this day was no exception. We hadn't yet bought West Grove but the strange experiences were already starting.

I'd fallen sound asleep, the minute I'd flopped into bed.

Until, that is, I was woken out of my very heavy sleep by the feeling that something was moving on my pillow behind me.

I froze.

It took several seconds for my sleep fog to disperse and for my mind to rationalise what I was experiencing.

The only way to describe it is to ask you to imagine a cat walking slowly on your pillow, while your head is on it. It's that feeling of the pillow moving slightly, like something is making an indent, so your head is moving slightly with each step.

The problem was we didn't have a cat. In fact, we didn't have a pet of any kind.

My mind started working overtime and, believe it or not, I was too scared to look. My mind was screaming out to turn around – but at the same time, screaming out to not turn around. I wanted to see what was there but was too scared of what I might see on the pillow.

I laid there for what seemed like an age, frozen with fear – and I'm not exaggerating when I say that. You know the saying, 'your hair stands on end with fear'? Well, it's spot on.

You may be thinking 'Martin was next to you, you weren't alone. Why didn't you wake him?'. But he was well out of it, lucky him.

My mind was creeping me out. I was attempting to pluck up the courage to have a look at what was there, but I imagined turning around and being confronted with a scary face or creature – and then what would I do? That thought was enough to stop me from looking.

I must have finally fallen asleep because the next thing I knew, I was waking up and it was morning. I immediately relayed the tale to Martin. He listened but couldn't add anything by way of explanation, and I think he may have thought I was dreaming (I categorically wasn't).

I ran this over in my mind repeatedly throughout the day, I knew I'd been awake. Besides, I'd been in a deep sleep, and then, in an instant, I wasn't. When I think about it now, it doesn't sound remotely scary. But I can assure you that it was, and it affected me significantly. I became increasingly scared to go to sleep, because that strange sensation continued for many years.

One year, we travelled to Turkey and had a fabulous holiday. But while we were there, the same thing happened. I was woken out of a deep sleep with the feeling of something walking behind me on the pillow.

As crazy as this sounds, it felt so much like a creature walking on my pillow that I considered whether our childhood pet cat Smokey, who had died several years before, had come back. After all, Smokey had enjoyed sleeping on my pillow at night.

Even though that thought popped into my mind, I was still scared. So much so, that I moved off the pillow and laid completely under the covers. I was wide awake with fear, my mind racing, and it was so hot. If you've ever been to Turkey, you'll know just how hot! It was really off the scale. But I stayed there all night, not daring to emerge.

What made this incident so scary was being unable to fathom why, as I was abroad, this thing had followed me? I know my thoughts sound irrational but I'm relaying how it made me feel at the time.

It was a feeling that returned repeatedly over the following years but in a way that became more significant, as I'll explain later in this saga.

Chapter 13

The old warehouse that housed the gym still retained its industrial character, with concrete floors, metal girders and pillars, and bare brick walls, all adding to the unique atmosphere.

It was a sizeable place and drew many positive comments over the years. Hence Brendan Monks' comment, when he visited for my photoshoot, that it was one of the best gyms he had been in. A compliment indeed.

Several years in, we were going from strength to strength, establishing our name and a reputation for producing champions. There was constant local media attention, and business and life were good.

The reception area was staffed by a fabulous team and, on occasion, me. I enjoyed meeting new people and supporting the team.

But there was something a little odd taking place. This is how it began...

We had an outside agency spend a few weeks in the club to promote the gym and support our efforts to introduce new members. It was going well. At all times, as least one of the promotional staff would be in reception, greeting any visitors as soon as they came in.

Behind reception was the ladies-only toning table area. The main gym entrance was at the bottom of the stairs and if the door was left open, it could be a draughty area.

One day, I was passing through reception and the staff member on duty was sitting in a slightly odd place: on a chair, in the doorway to the toning table room. She was in sight, but it was a strange place to sit, so I asked her why she was there.

"I'm not going to sit on reception," she replied.

"Is it because you're cold?" I asked.

"No, I've just had a pen thrown at me."

I started laughing. I honestly thought she was joking. But she wasn't.

"What do you mean, you've just had a pen thrown at you?" I asked. I didn't mean to sound patronising, but I thought she was making things up. Frankly, I thought at first that she was being a bit weird.

Why would anyone throw a pen at her? And how could anyone have thrown a pen at her? The reception counter consisted of two shelves, the lower of which was wider than the other, to enable the team to sit at it and use it as a desk area. The signing in book and pen simply sat on the top shelf, so people could use it easily.

I thought perhaps a pen had rolled off the counter and she either hadn't realised what had happened or was exaggerating. Either way, it didn't make any sense.

She simply repeated that a pen had been thrown at her. She was able to meet and greet from her unusual location, so it wasn't necessarily a problem. I went on my way with a smile, still thinking that she was imagining things.

The promotion continued for a further two weeks, and whenever she was on duty, she'd sit in the doorway.

Shortly afterwards, one Friday afternoon, I was standing behind the reception counter with Jamie, one of the gym managers, and my middle daughter Lydia (who did a fabulous job, by the way).

I recalled what the promo woman told me and asked the others what they thought. Lydia and I were open-minded, but Jamie was absolutely, argumentatively, adamantly in denial that this could have taken place. He insisted that she was obviously making it up or exaggerating what had happened.

"So," I asked him, "Do you have a completely closed mind then?"

"Well, yes," he answered.

"Do you believe in ghosts?"

"Absolutely not," he replied firmly.

I mentioned, without going into detail, that I'd had experiences and therefore kept an open mind. I'd had no idea, when I started this conversation, that he would get so heated about it.

As he fiercely stated, he was an absolute non-believer in anything 'paranormal'. His closed mind was his prerogative though, so I changed the subject, keen to lighten the atmosphere. Little did we know at the time that his words were to come back and bite him...

By coincidence, his extraordinary experience happened on another Friday afternoon. There we were again, all three of us, behind the reception counter. We were chatting away about anything and everything, laughing and joking and generally having a good time.

Jamie and I were standing up, and Lydia was sitting down. Out of nowhere, the pen on the counter rose about a foot in the air and stayed there for what was probably a split second

– but seemed a long time. Then, it was thrown violently downwards, hitting the lower desk, before bouncing off and hitting me in the leg.

Without any exaggeration, all three of us froze! We just stood (or sat) open-mouthed.

I was the first to break the silence.

"Right," I said, "I know what I saw, but I want you guys to tell me what just happened."

They both described the same events.

Instantly, I looked at Jamie and said, "Explain."

"I can't."

"But Jamie, you're an absolute non-believer in anything paranormal, so I'd like you to tell us or deny what has just happened."

His response? "I can't deny it, because I've just seen it, but I also can't explain it."

He was red in the face and had a shocked expression, that was, maybe, a little embarrassed too, given the previous conversation on this matter.

We stood for a minute or so, faintly smiling at one another, each of us lost in our thoughts about what had occurred. Then we simply continued about our business. Jamie took himself off into the weights room and I left Lydia to continue working on reception. Thankfully, she was happy to do that.

As far as I know, the incident with the pen was never repeated but just a few weeks later, there was to be another strange occurrence around the reception area.

Let me explain the layout of the reception area, as it is pertinent.

If you were to enter the gym and sign in at reception, you would either turn left, towards the ladies-only area or right, to go into the mixed training spaces.

Immediately before the ladies-only area, there was a small room with seating and frosted glass windows, where visitors would wait to be seen. The frosted glass windows formed part of the corridor, so when anyone was walking in this section of the corridor, people in reception could see them through the frosted glass.

On this particular day, Lydia was on reception again. One of the members had finished training and was in the waiting room, knowing his wife would emerge from the ladies only area and would come through that way before leaving the club.

The door that separated the ladies' facilities from the corridor was heard to close. A second or two later, a figure walked past the frosted glass, and so he stood up to greet his wife. He waited, as did Lydia, who knew her and wanted to speak to her.

Nobody appeared.

"That's odd," he said to Lydia.

"I know. Where is she?"

He went through the waiting room and walked into the corridor. A few seconds later, he returned to the room on his own.

"She isn't there."

Lydia agreed. Several minutes later, his wife finally appeared but none of them had an explanation for what had happened.

Go figure!

Unfortunately, the mystery didn't end there. Another Friday afternoon – it was always a quiet time, so maybe that explains why these things seemed to happen then.

It was my turn to work on reception. Just as the man waiting for his wife did, I heard the door close and naturally waited for that person to come out. It became a habit – you'd have a chat or simply say goodbye.

Again, like Lydia and the man, I waited. And I waited some more, before curiosity got the better of me and I got up and went to look in the corridor. There wasn't anyone to be seen.

Where did they go? There wasn't anywhere for them to go other than to leave!

This was to become a regular occurrence when I did my shift on reception on those quiet Friday afternoons – and there was more.

Our youngest daughter Aaron, who was just five years old at the time, would spend a lot of her non-school time with us at the gym. We had ample space for her to play close to us and we had our private area, including a fully fitted kitchen and lounge area with satellite TV, so she was well taken care of. When I was covering reception, she would be in the private space with Martin and, as a sociable little girl, she sometimes spent time chatting to the members, who enjoyed her company.

One afternoon, I heard her in the club, running around the reception. I could hear her little feet pattering up and down, so I called out to her to come round to where I was and stop running about.

She didn't stop running – and she didn't respond either. I asked her again. The same response. I admit, by then I was getting a little annoyed, so I stopped what I was doing, and got up and walked around the other side of the counter to tell her.

She wasn't there.

I walked into the waiting room area and the corridor, but she wasn't there either. I left reception and walked through the toning table room, which led to our private space.

And there she was, in the lounge area with Martin.

"Has Aaron just come back in here?" I asked.

"No, why?" replied Martin.

"Oh, it doesn't matter. I just thought she was running around reception."

I went back, puzzling over what had just occurred. I knew I'd heard what I'd heard and hadn't imagined it – but could I be sure?

Well, it happened again. That solved my fears that I was going mad, but it presented another problem: there was something strange going on.

Suffice to say, this became a regular occurrence on my Friday afternoon shift.

The next time I heard the running feet, I investigated again. There was no-one there. I felt a shiver down my spine and goose pimples on my skin, but over time, I became quite used to it and would just ignore the noises. I had the impression that a young child was present, for whatever reason – I can't explain why but that's how it felt.

Around this time, we decided it would be a positive move to live in the gym. The facilities were already there, so it wasn't any hardship. In fact, it made things a whole lot easier. We worked long hours and were committed to our coaching roles, which took us to boxing shows around the country on evenings and weekends. We'd often arrive home in the early hours of the morning. We were literally only sleeping there, so it made good sense to move, and it worked out very well.

We made our space at the gym very comfortable (it was quite a hike to visit the toilet during the night, but needs must!), so on most nights we fell into bed, exhausted, and slipped into a deep sleep.

This night started the same way, but it was to be different to any that had gone before.

I came out of a deep sleep by sitting up and calling out for Martin. I didn't wake up first and then consciously shout. That wouldn't have necessarily been so strange. Rather, I sat up, called out and only then became aware that I'd done it. It felt very strange.

I recall thinking, in that foggy way when you've been woken out of deep sleep and don't know where you are or what day it is, that I didn't know where Martin was. And why the hell had I just sat up and shouted his name?

I got out of bed tentatively and walked into the next room, which led through to the boxing gym. Martin was standing there in the moonlight, looking bemused.

"Martin! What's wrong?"

"It's very strange Anne," he said. "I got up to go to the loo and when I walked into here, I saw a young boy in the corner of the room. He was kind of glowing in white light, but I didn't think anything of it. In my sleep-like state I walked towards him and instinctively bent down to pick him up. When I did that, he disappeared."

"Wow! How weird is that? How strange too, that I sensed you were frightened. I was fast asleep – I didn't even know you'd got out of bed!"

Martin told me he hadn't been frightened but became aware of what he was doing when he heard me call. It was as though I had woken him out of a trance. He'd heard me shout just as he was sweeping his arms around the young boy.

It was almost unbelievable, but we had to believe it because we'd just had the experience.

Martin took himself to the loo and I went back to bed. It took a while for us to fall asleep, but the next day was another busy one, so we had little time to dwell on it.

Some months later, the thought popped into my head that perhaps the running feet sound was connected to this little boy. Had this child followed us to the gym? If so, why?

I didn't have any answers.

The experience was never repeated – but also never forgotten.

Chapter 14

We lived in the gym for two years. Although it had been a sensible move, it was an absolute joy to return to living like other people, in a regular home.

West Grove was still not on the horizon but our first night out of the gym felt like sleeping in a luxury hotel. Our en-suite bathroom wasn't exceptionally luxurious per se, but it certainly felt like it. I guess we'd got so used to living in a warehouse-style apartment attached to a nearly public facility.

We certainly didn't regret the move, and we settled back in very quickly. Life was good in every way, and the boxers continued to be successful, with more champions under our belt (pardon the pun).

We were once more like any regular married couple. And like any regular married couple, we sometimes fell out.

Typically, I can't for the life of me remember what we'd argued about that night, but we were lucky enough to have four bedrooms, so I took myself off to sleep in one of the others. As I settled in for the night, I don't mind admitting I was enjoying having space to myself, both literally and metaphorically.

All was well, until I woke up in the middle of the night with a feeling of being pushed out of bed.

I was a little panic-stricken, but I questioned it and I concluded that I'd been dreaming, albeit a rather strange dream.

I settled back down after a while, but as soon as I started to drift off back to sleep, it happened again.

This time, I was aware that I wasn't asleep, so I knew I wasn't dreaming. If I wasn't dreaming, then did I imagine this feeling? Twice?

A little scared, I got out of bed and turned on the light. I don't know why it was a frightening experience, but I was feeling frightened.

I lay still again, pondering things, and eventually drifted off to sleep once more. Yet again came the feeling of slowly being pushed out of bed. Well, this was becoming ridiculous, frightening, and annoying all at once. But fright was the predominant feeling, so I leapt out of bed and, swallowing my pride, went back to our bedroom. I was reluctant but it was my favoured option. I snuggled up to Martin and fell fast asleep.

In the morning, I attempted to explain but he was barely listening, and I think he assumed I was dreaming (as I did initially).

That was the end of that then. Except, it wasn't. This experience was to be repeated but not for a couple of years.

The next time was shortly after we'd moved into West Grove. Again, I'd had a fall out with Martin (it didn't happen often!) and taken myself off to a spare bedroom.

I'd slept for a couple of hours when I was woken up with the feeling of being pushed out of bed. This time I got up at the first push and turned on the light and the TV, before getting back into bed.

I was more fearful than the first time. I'm not sure if that was because we were in an older property, where we'd had other experiences. Or perhaps it was because it wasn't the first time this had happened. Anyway, I sat up watching TV for a while but eventually my eyelids began to close, and I started to drift off.

There it was again. That feeling of slowly being pushed out of bed. That was it. I leapt up, got back into my bed, and snuggled up to Martin.

Just like the first time, I mentioned it to him in the morning. He took more notice but neither of us had a rational explanation. Still, sharing the experience and being listened to was reassuring and I didn't tell anyone else what had happened.

It's not as though it's a typical, everyday conversation: "What unknown entity pushed you out of bed last night while you were sleeping?"

I was also conscious that we'd shared some of our experiences early on and one or two of our friends and family said they were a little nervous to visit, so we didn't talk as openly after that.

Fast forward several months. Our two eldest daughters, Dionne and Lydia, were visiting with their friends, for a girl's night in. These events were always such fun and the get-together was a complete success. We eventually made it to our beds, the girls having chosen their preferred bedrooms.

Morning came.

I went in to speak to Dionne, but she wasn't there. It was relatively early – too early for them to be up and about normally. But the bed had been slept in.

I immediately went to speak to Lydia and there they both were. They stirred as I went in, so I asked the obvious question.

"Why are you both in here?"

"Oh Mum, I was so scared," said Dionne. I was instantly concerned and guessed what might be coming, but I kept the thought to myself.

"I was lying in bed fast asleep," she continued, "and I thought I was dreaming that I was being pushed out of bed. It scared me, so I got up and turned the light on to make me feel less frightened and then got back into bed.

"I started to fall asleep but again I felt as though I was being pushed out of bed. I was so scared, Mum!"

I knew exactly how she felt. I had a dilemma: do I confess that this has happened to me several times and suffer their possible wrath that I hadn't warned them? Or do I keep quiet?

I kept quiet (well, until a later date when I felt it was more appropriate to confess).

"I can't explain how scared I was," said my daughter. "You don't need to," I thought. I didn't offer any explanation. I just listened.

"I'm not sleeping in there again Mum. I'm sorry but I just can't."

"It's OK, I understand," I told her. And I really did.

Part of me felt guilty about not having shared my experience before it happened to Dionne. But I told myself not to be so silly; there was a good reason I hadn't. I didn't want to frighten them or put ideas into their heads.

That rationale had backfired though.

I must admit that unless we were both imagining things, this demonstrated that my experiences had been 'real'.

Dionne and I now had a shared experience. But did that help explain what or why this was happening? In a nutshell, no.

Dionne wouldn't necessarily agree, but for me, it offered a little comfort that we'd both been through the same thing.

Later, when I talked to her about what had happened, she wasn't in the slightest bit angry with me and understood my reasoning.

Time passed. Dionne never slept in that room again, although it hasn't been mentioned again. Until now.

Chapter 15

It started out as an evening like any other.

Martin and I were in the lounge with the TV on, and our youngest daughter Aaron was in bed.

Suddenly something caught my eye. I thought I saw a bright, perfectly white, round object moving around the ceiling area. It was about the size of a small orange. It was a very quick glimpse and then it was gone.

An hour or so later, the same thing happened again. in a different part of the room. A bit distracting but I thought little of it.

Was I getting a migraine? It seemed unlikely because I've only ever had two in my life, and they were many years previously.

A few nights later, the same scene. And the circles of light appeared again. This time, they were sometimes white, with varying degrees of brightness. They were occasionally very small and then slightly larger. I followed one with my eyes as it floated across the ceiling. It was an iridescent blue.

What's happening?

It was slightly distracting, but I didn't speak out. After all, what was there to say?

But it continued. Night after night, day after day, week in week out, and yes, you've guessed it, month after month. It went on for years – so long that I couldn't possibly relate every single experience.

Eventually, I had to say something to Martin. As expected, he gave a slight laugh and asked what I was talking about.

I believe he was in denial. The truth was, he was a little scared by this and everything else that had gone on. I was sympathetic to that, and I also understood the adage 'seeing is believing'. If you don't see it, it doesn't exist.

Nonetheless, I knew I wasn't making it up, and at the risk of ridicule I wanted to share it. Besides, there was a small part of me that couldn't shake off the thought that maybe there was something wrong with my brain.

The longer it went on, the more worried I became about my brain health.

But that fear subsided greatly one evening.

We were both sitting in the lounge again; Martin on one sofa and me on the other, opposite each other. We were deep in conversation when, out of the blue, I saw a perfectly round, solid, shimmering silver ball, a little bigger than a tennis ball.

It was moving slowly from left to right, just about level with Martin's elbow, and gliding towards him.

I watched it as it moved towards him and remember thinking, "What on earth is that? Where on earth has it come from?"

It looked a little like when you blow bubbles and form a particularly large one.

Then I thought, "Is it going to touch Martin?"

But this time, to my relief and surprise, I noticed that as we were speaking, Martin's eyes moved from looking at me. He appeared to be following the silver ball.

I asked him outright.

"What are you looking at?"

He hesitated for a moment. "I've just seen a shimmering ball hovering in mid-air while moving towards me," he said. "It just appeared as we were speaking, and it was travelling about this height and moving towards me." He indicated the height and direction of travel.

"Yes!" I said, and jumped up off the sofa, with excitement. "Wow! So, you've seen what I've seen."

I can't emphasise enough how reassuring it felt that someone else had witnessed it too. And we had seen it together. I couldn't be imagining it; it couldn't be my brain. I distinctly remember thinking, "At least I'm not going mad."

With that, Martin got up from the sofa and left the room. I heard him walking up the stairs and a minute or so later, he reappeared with a camera in his hand. He started taking random photos of the room.

"What are you doing?" I asked him.

"I'm trying to get a picture of what we've just seen."

"That's hilarious! Let me get this straight Martin. I've been telling you for months – no, *years,* that I've been seeing things and you weren't interested. You didn't believe me and you absolutely wouldn't discuss it. And yet the very first time you see anything, you want photographic evidence!"

Why hadn't I thought of that?

Although he took several pictures, he didn't capture anything unusual.

We sat for a while, discussing what had just happened and how surprised we were that we had both experienced the same thing.

I have to say, though, I made the point more than once that he hadn't believed me when I had mentioned my experiences. Was he now in agreement with me?

Of course, he was. He couldn't deny this any longer.

The evening ended without any further sightings or strange anomalies, and we went to bed.

I had a smile on my face though. Martin would now find it impossible to deny what I was seeing, and I took some comfort from that.

Even though he'd tried to take pictures, it didn't occur to me, at this time, to do the same. It was to be several years before I started taking photographs, and there was a more profound reason for doing so. But I'll come to that a little later.

It never entered our minds to wonder what the ball of light was. That may sound a little strange now, but we knew we had both seen a shimmering ball. Questioning what it was came later too.

Chapter 16

It was around this time that I received a telephone call with devastating news.

It was very close to Christmas. School was closed and my youngest daughter Aaron and I had spent many pleasant hours filling our home with decorations. We had several Christmas trees, and the finishing touch was a sparkly one in her bedroom, adorned with petite ballerina figures, small stuffed animals, and tiny wrapped parcels.

We were delighted with our efforts, and she could hardly contain her excitement. She would have been very happy to have seen Santa there and then. But of course, like all children, she had to wait just a little bit longer.

At this point, she was in the second year of primary school. She loved it and so did we, especially her form teacher, Mrs C. What a remarkable teacher and human being!

It was partly thanks to her enormous efforts that the school existed at all. She was a tiny bundle of absolute joy and knowledge.

The ethos was that the children remained with the same teacher throughout their school life, and I was especially pleased about that because Aaron's teacher, without doubt, was one of the best.

The moment I met her, I felt an immediate connection. I can't explain how or why. The best I can manage is that it felt as though I had always known her. We got along like a house on fire. It made my day when it was my turn to collect Aaron from school, because I could snatch a few moments with her.

Parents' evenings were delightful. The time would be spent briefly catching up with Aaron's progress and then the remaining time spent chatting. To be honest, Aaron was doing so well at school that there wasn't any need to ponder on specifics.

Mrs C had a terrific sense of humour; we laughed a lot. She was always proud to talk about her son, who worked as an Accident and Emergency doctor, in the south of England. She mentioned him often and was comical when explaining that he was a strapping young man over six feet tall – when she didn't even reach five feet. She had lived in Africa for many years; her husband was African, and her son had been born there.

My fondness for her meant it was very disturbing when I received a very strange message while at a friend's house one evening. My friend had engaged an experienced tarot reader and, although it was a fun night, when my turn arrived, I went in to see the woman with some trepidation.

That feeling didn't last for long, though. I soon relaxed and became gripped by her narrative. She hardly paused for breath and although I had a pen and paper to take notes, I was selective in my note taking, because she spoke quickly and precisely.

It was all so positive until she said that Aaron would be leaving her school. Never! It was a forceful 'never', too.

After that, I was distracted and couldn't focus on what she was telling me. My mind just lingered on the suggestion that Aaron would be changing schools. I couldn't see it happening.

My turn finished, and I rejoined my friends and shared some of the narrative before leaving for home.

The drive gave me time to reflect. I replayed her words around Aaron leaving school and sent up a prayer that she'd got that wrong.

We'd never want to take Aaron away from Mrs C. I was worried: surely Mrs C wasn't going to be ill? Or certainly not to the extent that Aaron would have to leave?

For the following few weeks, this snapshot of the narrative played on my mind. I even began to feel a little down about it. I truly didn't want Aaron to leave school. But some months passed, Aaron was happy and Mrs C wasn't ill.

On the final day of term, the children were all very excited for Christmas. I collected Aaron and gave Mrs C a gift. I'd bought her one of my favourite books and I was very excited for her to read it, hoping that she would share the pleasure of the experience.

She thanked me and said she would take it with her to open on Christmas day. She told me excitedly that she was heading south to visit her son, to spend precious time with him over the holidays.

I left with Aaron, feeling sad that it would be a couple of weeks before we'd see her again, but I wished her well.

In fact, I would never see her again.

When the head of the school phoned, I just knew what he was going to say. An overwhelming feeling of dread and a knowledge that Mrs C was no longer with us came over me, instantly.

"I am sorry, but I have some very sad news," said the headteacher. "Mrs C has been killed in a car accident."

I honestly can't remember what was said after that.

I felt sick. I cried. I had taken the call in our office at home, and I couldn't leave the room. I sobbed for 20 minutes before I finally stopped and even then, it took all my willpower to compose myself. I was so overwhelmed by the news.

I had to act bravely for Aaron. I had to tell her. But how do you tell a young child news like that?

Christmas was not the same that year and although I put on a brave face for my daughter, it was a real struggle. I felt utterly bereft.

It's true that time is a great healer, although it took many months before I had a day without being interrupted by thoughts of Mrs C. I would reflect on what we had shared. I missed her overwhelmingly. I still miss her. I was truly blessed to have known her.

Aaron didn't return to the school ever again. She couldn't face it. Most of the pupils in her class didn't go back, such was the strength of feeling for Mrs C.

It was a year or so later.

I was having a lengthy telephone conversation with my cousin, Jean. She lives in the south – Dorset to be precise – and as I'm up north, we don't often get to meet up.

When we were children though, my brother and I would spend most of our summer holiday with our cousins. My aunt and uncle's large bungalow in Bognor Regis was near the beach, so there was plenty of room for us all to stay. We have many fond memories of those times, and I can recall every detail of the house.

These days, Jean and I only talk on the phone a couple of times a year. I wish it was more, but our busy lives get in the way.

She's a few years older than me (hopefully she won't mind me mentioning that) but we've always been close. We share the same sense of humour, and we laugh and giggle a lot when we speak. It's always a pleasure and I feel such a bond with her that we often say we're more sisters than cousins.

Half an hour of chat had passed when I mentioned that I was managing to move on from the painful experience of Aaron's teacher's death. I mentioned her full name and Jean replied, quite rightly, that it was an unusual surname.

I continued, explaining how upset I had been, how special she was, and how much I missed her.

"How unusual," said Jean. "I know a doctor by that name."

"You do?"

"Yes, he works at the hospital."

"What? That's a coincidence."

"He's from Africa."

I nearly dropped the phone.

"Which hospital does he work at?"

Jean told me.

"It's him," I sobbed. "It's her son."

Jean worked as a midwife, so I assumed that was the link.

Once I'd composed myself, I asked, "How do you know him? Did you work with him?"

"No, Anne," and she continued with a bombshell that shook me to my core. "He bought Mum and Dad's house. You remember – the bungalow where we used to live when you came and stayed for the summers."

How could I forget? I couldn't speak.

When I finally found some words, I could only mutter, "What a coincidence!"

I cried for the fact that Mrs C wasn't with us any longer to share this amazing story. There was a connection after all, albeit tentative and indirectly via her son.

All I could imagine was me telling her this very strange coincidence and what we would have made of it, but I was no longer able to share it with her. I was so sad about what could have been, but I was comforted by the conclusion to this strange series of events.

Again, an experience that was almost beyond comprehension.

How could it be that I had met this beautiful soul, in the manner that I did, and that following her death, I discovered such a connection?

Chapter 17

I was by now seeing orbs constantly. So much so that sometimes, I'd leave the lounge for a brief period, to get a break from the distraction. They varied in size, luminosity and shade, varying from a dull white to a luminous white, or from pale lilac through to turquoise and aquamarine blue. They're not camera-shy either and I have many photos.

The orbs would sometimes appear for just a split second and sometimes stay around for several seconds; long enough for me to focus and, on occasion, follow them with my eyes as they travelled.

That said – and please bear with me on this – I'll try to explain how I 'saw' them.

I didn't see the orbs with my eyes. Obviously, you do see with your eyes, but it was as though they appeared as part of the periphery of what I was looking at. It was almost as if they were projected from my mind.

During this period, when the frequency of the appearance of orbs increased significantly, I became worried. I worried about my health – my brain health, to be precise. I began to be concerned that there was something not quite right with my brain or my eyesight. And it began to frequently dominate my thoughts.

It was a catch 22 situation.

One day I remember driving along in a daze, focused almost entirely on what I could do about checking out my eyesight or my brain health. I kid you not.

But I was too scared to make an appointment with the GP, just in case there *was* something wrong. Quite clearly, something was going on, but I didn't have the nerve to have that something investigated via the GP.

Eventually, though, I found the answer – and it arose most uncannily and unexpectedly (nothing new there!).

Alongside the increased sightings of the orbs was an increase in the occasions that I felt a presence on my bed. It wasn't a regular thing, but it was frequent enough to give me another thing to worry about.

It wasn't really worrying that I was imagining it though, because I came to know for sure that I wasn't.

How did I come to that conclusion? The frequency of these occurrences meant I was able to control my fear enough to question whether I was awake. I knew I was and therefore, I wasn't dreaming. I started to test myself and my awareness. I'd ask myself questions that I answered in my head, and I'd move my eyes on demand, so I knew I was in control.

But if I wasn't dreaming, then what? I was definitely feeling the movement on the bed.

The fundamental question was, why? Why was it happening?

I need to explain that I was scared every time. I was too scared to turn around – to this day, I've still never plucked up the courage. It's impossible to explain the fear.

Although I was no longer unduly concerned about my health or eyesight, as I was now confident that I was awake at such times, I was concerned about what or why these things were happening.

Fortunately, I was preoccupied with the business most of the time. Our boxers were phenomenally successful. A couple of them were now proudly wearing the GB shirt and boxing internationally. Wow!

The vision and ambitions we'd had were being met – and our competing lads were achieving their dreams too. Life was beyond good, but I couldn't shift my doubts. OK, I'd progressed to knowing I wasn't dreaming – but I still needed answers.

I needed to act to resolve the worry, once and for all.

But I didn't make an appointment with the GP. Instead, it was a business appointment that was to provide the insight I'd been looking for.

Chapter 18

A few weeks after Mrs C died, I struck up a conversation that was to put my mind at rest – and changed my thinking on many things.

Martin and I took it in turns to collect our youngest daughter, Aaron, from school. I enjoyed going, not only because I was excited to see her, but I was also excited to see Mrs C.

It was a small school, so we got to know most of the children by name, regardless of whether they were in the same class as our daughter. One young boy drew my attention, not just because he was such a handsome child, but because he spoke so eloquently. I would often hear him interact with his mum, but I had no real reason to speak to her because her son was in the year above Aaron.

Although it had felt intrusive to speak to her until now, I knew we'd share the common bond of missing Mrs C. One day, we passed in the street, so I said hello and we had a brief conversation about our mutual appreciation for our children's lovely teacher.

I also took the opportunity to tell her (as I'd so often wanted to do) how eloquent her son was and how much I'd enjoyed listening to him.

We chatted some more, and it transpired that she worked for a charity, supporting young people with disabilities. I was hopeful that we could offer sessions at our gym, giving the youngsters the chance to take part in activities they hadn't had access to before.

We arranged to meet formally to discuss funding for the idea.

A few days later, as I drove to her business premises, I passed the GP surgery and made a mental note to make that appointment and have my brain and eyesight checked out, once and for all.

I arrived, accepted her kind offer of a coffee and prepared to start the conversation about our idea. But before I could speak, she dropped a bombshell.

"Are you imagining someone lying on your bed?" she asked.

I was lost for words, although internally, I was thinking, "What? How? When? What's happening? How did you know?"

I was utterly flummoxed.

I believe I just sat there, shaking my head, thinking, "I'm here for a business meeting, you're a relative stranger – we've never spoken until the other day."

Even now, years later, I still find this experience hard to believe. But believe I must because it happened exactly as I have just described it.

Eventually, I recovered from the shock.

"How did you know?" I stammered.

"It's your dad."

Here we go again – completely and utterly shocked into silence.

I became mute.

"He's here now, a very handsome man," she continued. "He's standing next to you. He has a dog with him; a Labrador."

I was still mute. Yes, we did have a Labrador, our family pet, Shane, who had died years ago. And yes, Dad was handsome – in fact, he was often described as a Gregory Peck lookalike.

"I can't believe it," I remember saying. I also recall a profound feeling of both fear and relief.

I had the answer now. I didn't need to worry. I wasn't imagining these things and I didn't need to have my eyesight – or my head – tested.

How bizarre though. This relative stranger – because until that moment, that's what she was – answered my concerns in one fell swoop. She explained her gift of clairvoyance, we finished our meeting and said our goodbyes.

I will be forever grateful to her and her gift. The world works in mysterious ways, and it doesn't get much more mysterious than this.

Chapter 19

Once in a blue moon, we had a night out. Put the flags out!

It was rare that we could spare the time, what with running the business, coaching, and attending the amateur boxing competitions. But tonight was rather a special one – we'd planned a night out with a group of friends to watch an exciting evening of professional boxing.

It also made a change to dress in something other than gym clothes. That was a treat in itself! We visited a couple of bars before getting seated at the venue.

We were keen to see a specific US boxer, who, despite being a bit flashy and entering the ring flanked by showgirls, was very talented.

We were close to ringside, so it looked like we were in for a good night, with a great view of the action. And the atmosphere was electric. There was a local boxer on the card, and we were excited to see his fight too. It was close to Christmas, which seemed to add to the glamour of the occasion.

All was well. We were all enjoying the boxing and the occasion. The showgirls didn't disappoint – nor the boxing, so far. The local lad was up next, and he put up a great fight.

Then, in the final round of the 12-round bout, he was knocked out cold. He didn't get up.

It was a very distressing scene. The crowd was silent. The only sounds to be heard were hysteria and panic from his wife and brother, both ringside. It was a sickening sight and the distress of his wife and brother was devastating to witness.

After a few minutes, he was stretchered out of the ring. The night was over. We left.

The journey home was subdued. Although I didn't personally know the boxer or his family, I felt devastated for them.

I couldn't shake the sadness and went to sleep worrying whether he would survive. The images of his knockout and the distressing scenes that followed played repeatedly in my mind, like watching a movie of the event, over again.

I tried to imagine how his family members were dealing with the devastation. Finally, out of exhaustion, I slept.

When I woke the next morning, much to my delight, the overwhelming feeling of sadness had left me. And with profound reason. I just knew he was going to be OK.

How could I know? I had experienced a vivid dream. And like before, I knew it was more than a dream.

It started in a hospital corridor. I was there, leaning against the wall, but invisible to those around me. And I had a huge smile on my face. I sensed very strongly the emotion of elatedness emanating from me. I recalled vividly feeling a strong sense of happiness, even though I was dreaming.

Next, I was watching family members talking with hospital staff. Again, they were completely unaware of my presence. This scene continued for what seemed like a couple of minutes. I became aware that I was at the hospital that the boxer had been taken to, even though he wasn't in sight. The feeling of happiness turned into frustration and impatience, as I became desperate to tell the family, particularly his wife, that he was going to be OK.

The very next second, I was standing next to a phone hanging on the corridor wall. It rang and I picked it up. It was the doctor explaining that the boxer was going to be OK and to please tell his wife.

I turned towards her and simply repeated the message. With that, she hugged me and there were tears of joy running down both our faces. She turned and went towards the rest of her family, who all hugged and cried tears of joy too.

This scene also appeared to last for a couple of minutes and then I woke up.

That's it. It was a brief and simple dream, but for all its simplicity, when I woke up, I felt overwhelmed with a sense of happiness and a conviction that he was going to live. It was a complete 360-degree turnaround from the previous evening's feeling of utter sadness.

I didn't immediately say anything about the dream to Martin. It didn't feel appropriate and besides, he would surely think I was going mad. I had no personal connection to the family. What would be the point?

It was especially frustrating to me at the time because I had mixed feelings. Should I reach out to the family and tell them that I knew he was going to be OK, despite the poor prognosis? How could I do that? Who would I speak to? And even if I could, would I be giving them false hope?

I simply couldn't take the chance.

The next evening, the story was on the news. The report conveyed the seriousness of the injury and the fact that the boxer was in a coma, with expectations of a very poor outcome. I couldn't contain myself and I told Martin about the dream and my confidence that, despite these reports, he was going to live.

I smiled through his negative comments – and I didn't blame him for them. I recognised that I probably sounded ridiculous, and I knew that only time would tell.

Time did tell. The boxer recovered.

There is an epilogue to this story.

A year or so later, Martin and I were at a boxing tournament in Hull, being held at St Paul's Gym. The competition was underway and because I wasn't in the corner for our boxers that day, I was sitting ringside.

I looked round and the boxer who had been knocked out came into the room. I was delighted to see him and to witness the great progress he had made with his recovery, but I was experiencing very mixed emotions.

I was struggling to comprehend that he was there, just a few feet away from me, and I'd experienced that dream and the message within it. But he had no awareness of that. I felt as though I knew him and had a connection with him, but he was completely oblivious. It was a very strange feeling indeed.

He received rapturous applause, which was well deserved. He made his way to the seating area and sat next to me. Just when I thought it couldn't get any stranger, it had.

Now, I was flummoxed. Simply because of the proximity, he turned to me and smiled and said hello.

What do I do – other than say hello in return?

I wanted to tell him about my dream and how I knew that he was going to live. I wanted to hug him and shake his hand.

I felt an amazing connection, I truly felt as though I knew him like a long, lost friend.

But, of course, I didn't tell him. The fact is, I didn't really know him. I didn't hug him or shake his hand. How could I?

I just sat, so distracted by his presence that I was oblivious to the boxing. After a while, I settled, and it became easier to resist the urge to speak to him.

After he left, I slightly regretted not talking to him. But the feeling didn't last long. Although I've never forgotten the experience, it's probably best to let sleeping dogs lie.

Chapter 20

Not every visitor had an extraordinary experience when visiting or staying over at West Grove, but usually, by nightfall, the conversation would lean towards the unusual events that had taken place over the years.

Often, we'd discuss the general subject of ghosts, and I always enjoyed these conversations. It was interesting to share the experiences and opinions of others and while I didn't want to bore anyone, my narrative was always well received, even by the non-believers.

I believe it's a positive thing to be cynical and I'm not on any soapbox to plug the truth of the paranormal. Each to their own. That said, I wouldn't be true to myself if I was in denial about my experiences.

However, my son-in-law, Mark, was particularly cynical. He found the whole subject of ghosts and the paranormal hilarious.

He couldn't take any discussion on the topic seriously, and, quite honestly, there wasn't any convincing him at all. He would politely listen to the telling of the latest tale but other than that he wasn't interested.

We had family get-togethers regularly. The grandchildren, nieces and nephews in the family, always had fun and this evening was no exception. The adults were scattered around the house, some playing games in one room and others elsewhere, listening to music. The party was in full swing. It was past the children's bedtime, but they were having fun, so it was going to be a late night for all.

Most people had gathered in the dining room or kitchen. I fancied a little peace, so I walked into the quietness of the lounge. Mark joined me, and we stood together, by the patio doors, looking out into the garden, chatting generally.

Directly opposite the patio doors, some 50 feet away, with an uninterrupted view, is a wooden cabin. It's usually used as a games room and bar, but it was too cold this evening, so everyone was in the house.

We were mid-conversation when a figure appeared. When I say figure, it was unlike any figure I'd seen before. This apparition appeared to be approximately seven feet tall, well-built, and dark brown. The only way I can describe it is if you imagine Superman in a costume that's head to toe dark brown, as opposed to the usual blue and red. That goes some way to describing what I saw.

The shoulders and head of the apparition were somewhat misty – although a very thick mist. The edges of the shoulders and head were blurred with a fog-like material that emanated in whispery shapes, like flames. The rest of the figure was solid and the contour of the head was distinguishable.

The figure appeared in front of the cabin door as though it had just stepped out, although the door didn't open. It walked a few paces straight ahead, head slightly bent downwards as though looking at the floor, before striding off to the left. After about half a dozen steps, it disappeared – literally!

Mark and I looked at each other. I knew he'd seen what I'd seen.

Careful not to describe the apparition, as I didn't want to influence him, I asked, "Did you just see something?"

"Yes," he answered.

"What was it?"

"I just saw a dark figure come out of the cabin."

Oh my God. The cynic had seen it too! As we were speaking, my sister-in-law, Andrea, came into the room. I turned to her and told her we'd just seen something strange in the garden.

I turned back to Mark.

"OK," I told him. "Before you say anything further, I want to ask you this. On the count of three, I want you to say which way the figure walked after appearing in front of the cabin. Don't say anything yet – I want to see if you saw exactly what I saw."

I counted to three.

"To the left," we said in unison.

I asked him if he was still a non-believer.

"Erm, I don't know," he replied.

I asked him to describe it in detail. It was exactly as I'd seen.

"Explain it then!" I challenged.

"I can't."

Well, neither could I.

Now it was my turn to laugh. Yet again, there didn't appear to be any rhyme or reason for what had happened. Another one for the record – and still, to this day, unexplained.

Also for the record, I was remarkably calm about the whole experience. I think it's because it happened outside the house. If it had gone on inside, I'd have been most concerned.

One dark evening, many months later, Andrea and I ventured into the garden for the sole purpose of attempting to capture something on camera. We did – and all will be revealed later. Although, it's what we didn't get on camera that shocked us the most.

CHAPTER 18 Two days before I'd had the overwhelming sense of love, several anomalies appeared. Uncannily, this photo was taken on 10 February 2016 at 7.32pm and the 'sense of love' picture below was taken at precisely the same time, 7.32pm, two days later. Coincidence?

CHAPTER 18 *"I felt an overwhelming sense of love"*. There appeared an outline of a figure in a long, sheer, flowing dress. The bodice shape can be seen clearly in the original image, the outline of the shape clearly seen in front of the cards. The dress dissipates into the floor. It's clear that the image is in front of the background, although it doesn't block the view of what's happening behind. This was the gel-like presence I'd been sensing for hours.

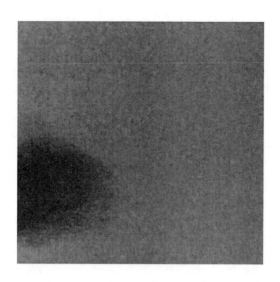

CHAPTER 21 *"It was a shock to zoom in on the 'blob'."*

CHAPTER 21 *"It isn't every day that the dogs would refuse to enter the hall".*

CHAPTER 23 *"Martin often used to wake with a feeling that he was being watched"*. I'd felt a presence on the landing and our bedroom door would regularly be open when we woke. This appears to be a large orb in my bedroom doorway. I was standing facing into the room when I took the photo, having sensed something present. This orb is like that in the lounge, taken some days prior to the appearance of the figure. (See Chapter 18).

CHAPTER 24 *Alongside the increased sightings of the orbs, was an increase in the occasions that I felt a presence on my bed.*

"If there's anyone there, come and sit on the bed."

What better way to reassure myself that I wasn't going crazy than to gather (or at least attempt to gather) photographic evidence?

CHAPTER 26 *"A long line of cloudy white misty cylindrical shapes. "There!" I would say and Andrea would point the camera in the right direction."*

CHAPTER 28 *"It became the norm for me to take photos"*, particularly as I was mostly home alone and experiencing these events on my own. I was sensing something in my bedroom, so I took a photo. The large orb appeared, the image shows movement and a denser centre, and to put the size in perspective, it's useful to compare this with the chest of drawers and the cushions on the floor.

CHAPTER *28 "It became the norm for me to take photos"*. Well, that's one way to light up a room. It's clear that the orb exhibits its own velocity, light source, and transparency.

CHAPTER 28 "*I jumped out of my skin.*" Incidentally, the image of me is blurred, having been captured mid-jump.

CHAPTER 30 *"As usual, on my birthday I was thinking of Dad."* As both my parents have now passed, I call out to them both on my birthday. I like to think they join us for our family celebration. This photo was taken when I was retiring to bed. It shows two mist-like shapes, of clearly different sizes. Mum was much shorter than Dad.

CHAPTER 33 *"Wow! As she was speaking, we all saw a very bright, white light"*. *"Lo and behold, the first photo exposed an unmistakable anomaly."*

Chapter 21

Some months passed, and things were unusually settled. Until, that is, they weren't.

When I say things were settled, I mean apart from the fact that I was seeing orbs floating around on a nightly basis. These were around the lounge predominantly but infrequently, I would also notice them in the dining room, kitchen and hall. So, apart from that, things were settled.

As I mentioned, West Grove is a substantial Victorian house, built in 1868, with a basically square layout that's typical of its era. My and Martin's bedroom was opposite our daughter Aaron's, with an en-suite bathroom in between, separating the rooms.

Because we had extensive land around the house and no close neighbours, we'd invested in an expensive alarm system, to give us peace of mind. It was on an electrical circuit that operated around the perimeter of the home, so the upstairs windows could be left open slightly on a warm evening, but as soon as the window was moved, it would trigger the alarm.

The alarm obviously made a very loud noise. We'd also paid extra to have a monitor in the hall, through which the operatives could communicate with us and check everything was OK if the alarm was set off. If they didn't get a response, they'd alert the police.

One night, I woke up needing to visit the loo. Martin and Aaron were fast asleep as I quietly but sleepily left the bedroom to get to the bathroom.

I stepped onto the landing and froze. I couldn't take another step.

Was I seeing things? Or was there a man with his back to me, creeping down the stairs?

He was heading down to the half-landing, where the stairs turned and descended to the hall. The half-landing featured a beautiful, arched stained glass window and I could see him clearly, although I was, by now, wondering if I was dreaming.

I stood, rooted to the spot. I was afraid and my sleepy brain was whirring. What would happen if I shouted out at him, and he turned around? What would I do then? If I woke Martin, would he rush out and get involved in a fight?

He certainly looked very real. I can still describe him to this day: rather short, about five and a half feet tall, with sandy hair that was quite short and wavy. He was wearing blue denim jeans and an olive-green bodywarmer.

He was creeping down the top stairs, relatively close to me. Had he heard me get out of bed and open the bedroom door?

I told myself that I must be dreaming and continued to the bathroom. After going to the loo, I had second thoughts and was too scared to leave the room.

My imagination started to get the better of me.

What if he had heard me and he was standing on the other side of the door, waiting for me to come out? What if he was a ghost, despite the modern-day clothes?

I wasn't thinking straight. I waited, for what felt like an age, plucking up the courage to leave. I could have just shouted for Martin, but I was loath to do that because I didn't want to make a fuss if I'd imagined it all.

Eventually, I took a deep breath and opened the door. The coast was clear – phew!

I distinctly remember that I walked ever so quickly, and sideways, so that I couldn't catch even the tiniest glimpse behind me. I got to the bedroom and shut the door behind me without turning around at all.

I stood and waited, breathing rather heavily. I waited a little longer but didn't hear a thing. I got into bed and, after a while, fell into a deep sleep until morning.

In the morning, I told Martin about the strange turn of events.

"You were dreaming," he insisted. "But why didn't you wake me? Don't deal with anything like that on your own again."

"I was worried about what would happen if I woke you," I replied. "Besides, I'm not sure if I was imagining it because I'd just woken up! But I must confess, it did all seem very real."

Martin got up and checked the whole house for any sign of burglary. Of course, the alarm hadn't gone off, but he made sure there were no signs of forced entry or windows being open. Eventually, he was satisfied that there wasn't anyone that could have entered during the night.

For the next day or so, I mulled over the incident and couldn't really come to any conclusion one way or another. Eventually it faded from my mind, and I stopped wondering how I could have seen a stranger in our home.

And then, a couple of weeks later, something similar happened.

It was a Saturday morning; I recall that vividly because we got to have a lie-in and didn't have to do the school run. I was first up as usual, making a pot of tea to take back to bed.

Strange – the back door was wide open. I closed and locked it. I looked around but didn't notice anything untoward. There didn't appear to be a thing out of place.

As the kettle boiled, I went into the office, a small room tucked away off the hall, to get the laptop. It wasn't there. I was sure I'd left it on the desk. Then it dawned on me.

"Martin!" I shouted up the stairs, "I think we've been burgled."

He immediately came down and we looked in all the downstairs rooms. There didn't seem to be anything amiss. It was then that I started looking in the office cabinet and drawers.

My bag was missing. Oh, why had I left it downstairs?

We realised then that we had, indeed, been burgled. It was a shock. How had it happened?

I was sure we'd locked the door the previous night and the key was still in the lock. It seemed that whoever had been there had left that way.

With that, we went upstairs and noticed that the side of the bath in the en-suite looked a little muddy. Taking a closer look, we saw that the window was slightly ajar. Sure enough, there were a couple of dirty footprints in and on the edge of the bath.

The burglar must have climbed in through the window, stood on the bath, walked out of the bathroom, and crept down the stairs.

Wow – surely not? I remembered my dream. Could it have been a premonition? Had we been warned?

Although we were both feeling angry and upset, these feelings were mixed with complete and absolute shock that what had transpired was likely to have been connected to what happened a couple of weeks earlier.

But it wasn't the time for figuring out the strange details. We called the police. They did what they had to do and explained it was unlikely that any fingerprints would be found, and therefore there was little chance that anyone would be arrested for the burglary.

They were right.

There wasn't any positive conclusion, other than the insurance company did their bit and we chalked the whole incident up to experience.

Footnote: Guess where my handbag is every evening at bedtime, these days?

Footnote 2: Why hadn't the alarm worked? It was still enabled the next morning!

Chapter 22

Years pass and much of the same thing occurs; seeing orbs in various rooms (particularly in the lounge where they appear regularly) and feeling something on the bed, although other experiences are few and far between.

Our youngest, Aaron, is growing into a loving and productive adult and enjoying her life. She's in a relationship and her boyfriend, Rob, is a welcome part of the family. He stays over regularly and is now familiar with some of our stories relating to our unusual experiences. Although he's a non-believer, he tries to keep an open mind. Aaron doesn't believe either, although she can't explain the ghostly figure in her bedroom a significant number of years ago.

What has changed though, is the fact that when I sense a presence, I now reach for the phone and take photos. That's very much thanks to Martin reaching for his camera after his first experience.

At times, these presences are more prevalent than others – usually when I have a period of several days of consistent and more intense visualisation of orbs. Initially, I didn't expect to see anything on the photos, because at some level I was still convincing myself that I wasn't seeing anything at all.

Well, part of me knew I was 'seeing' something, but I'd flit back and forth between certainty and doubt; thinking that perhaps this sort of thing happens as one gets older. I wondered if maybe the brain, or a problem with my eyesight, caused these sparks of light to appear. Don't laugh, I'm only being honest in stating what was going through my mind.

I can't stress enough that I was mulling this over every day – every spare minute. I'd think about it when driving the car or washing the pots, doing the laundry and so on, because it was difficult to always share these experiences with others. At the very least, I didn't want to bore them to death and, more seriously, I didn't want to frighten them away from visiting. Besides, like everyone, my life was busy, so I frequently kept my thoughts to myself. But that didn't stop them going around and around in my head.

One day stands out and is worthy of a mention.

By this time, I was caring for Brad, who had been part of our foster family for several years.

He'd decided to go to a friend's house after school for a few hours and, although it was early evening, the short winter days meant it was becoming dark outside.

I was watching TV as usual and relaxing without a thought in the world about seeing orbs, which hadn't appeared so far this evening. But then, very slowly, I became aware that something was distracting me.

Initially, I didn't really notice it. Then, I wasn't sure if I was imagining it.

It's very difficult to find the words to use to adequately describe what I'm trying to explain, but I want to convey what I was experiencing.

Anyway, here goes.

There appeared to be a clear, gel-like substance moving from one end of the room to the other. It was as though someone was walking back and forth along the room in front of me, roughly four or five feet away. The 'gel' was about six feet high and about four feet wide.

What could it be – and why was I seeing it?

Just as if someone was there, when the 'gel' passed in front of the TV screen, my view would be blocked for a moment.

It's so difficult to explain how I was watching TV and not really noticing that this was happening. I remember it was an hour or so into the experience before I was distracted to the point that I became aware.

I guess that proves I wasn't thinking about experiencing anything other than relaxing and watching TV.

I started to follow the abstracted movement with my eyes, whenever I noticed it. It wasn't constant – maybe every 15 minutes or so.

Slowly, a more defined outline of the shape began to appear. The only way I can describe it is that it seemed to have a thin line around it, or a more solid appearance at the edges.

At that point, I vividly recall feeling slightly nervous, although I wasn't sure why. The feeling intensified as the gel-like mass appeared again, but this time, it was very close to me. So much so that I leaned back and pushed myself into the sofa, trying to distance myself from it. It was almost in my face.

That was too much. I was home alone and, given my past experiences, I started to feel a little spooked out. I didn't want to leave the lounge, although I was afraid to stay there!

Thankfully, I didn't have to wrestle with this dilemma for long.

There was a loud knock at the door. It was Brad's annoying signature knock, which always sounded like he was about to break the door down. Whenever I spoke to him about his knock, he used to explain that it's a big house and I couldn't always hear him knocking. He had a point.

Anyway, that day, I was relieved to hear it. I knew I wasn't going to be alone.

I didn't say anything about it because I didn't want to frighten him. Not that he necessarily would be afraid – he was the usual non-believer who thinks something only exists if they've seen it with their own eyes. And that was fair enough.

I went back into the lounge and resumed watching TV, while he went up to his room and started gaming.

Sure enough, within a minute or so, there it was again. The 'gel' was back.

"This is ridiculous," I thought to myself and reached for my phone. I had to take a picture.

I was sure there wouldn't be anything unusual in the picture, but maybe it would reassure me. I knew what I was seeing but was I seeing it because I'd talked myself into it?

There was only one way to find out. I took a picture and was instantly shocked.

There was something. I hadn't imagined it.

"Oh my god!"

Mixed with the excitement of that discovery was an overwhelming sense of love. As I took the photo, I saw what appeared in the frame. Lit up by the flash of the camera, it suddenly became clear and obvious. The feeling of love overwhelmed me in that instant, and I started to cry tears of joy.

I couldn't contain the feeling, nor could I explain where it had come from. It lasted no more than a minute, but it was significant.

I appreciate that it all sounds ridiculous. It's not your everyday experience but I wouldn't be true to myself if I didn't tell the story.

It took me a couple of minutes to recover enough to attempt to rationalise the experience – and the photo. I leapt off the sofa and ran up the stairs. I knocked on Brad's door and entered the room, with no attempt to contain my excitement.

"What's going on?" he asked.

"I think I've seen something." I deliberately didn't go into detail. I wanted to truly test whether there was anything significant to see, or whether it was my imagination.

"Look at this photo and tell me if you can see anything."

He looked, he saw, and he described exactly what I had seen.

I've provided the picture, so you can see for yourself what was captured and make your own mind up.

It was a profound moment and there wasn't any going back from there on. Taking photos when I felt something significant became the norm, and whatever was materialising didn't let me down.

This experience overwhelmed me for several days, for what I hope are obvious reasons.

Chapter 23

As I mentioned in the previous chapter, my youngest daughter Aaron was a non-believer. She steadfastly refused to accept that orbs captured in photos were anything other than dust – the usual line when cynics are challenged with photographic evidence. But neither dust nor bugs are usually a valid explanation for the orbs.

Of course, I respected her opinion and although her experience of seeing the young girl in her room had been significant, it was a one-off event. An amount of cynicism is healthy, and to be expected, given that she had studied the sciences as part of her education.

But this was all about to change.

The first sign of a sea change was when she mentioned, on a couple of occasions, that she was seeing things out of the corner of her eye. I was quite excited but didn't openly say that because I didn't want to influence her.

There were to be significant sightings later and I'll get to that. But at this point, one event stands out as exceptional in that it was validated – although not by humans.

It was the weekend. We were all at home, and my daughter, her partner and I were sitting in the lounge. Brad, the young man I was caring for, was upstairs in his room, gaming.

We were chatting generally and if I recall, choosing a film to watch later.

A rescue dog had joined our family by then, and he was asleep near us, alongside my other daughter's dog, which we were looking after while she was away.

I hadn't meant to get a dog! I'd recently been to Spain on a short break with some girlfriends. It was the first time we'd all been away together, and we had had a great time. One of the friends had a villa out there, so she was a regular visitor and would often help at the local dog sanctuary.

Volunteers were desperately needed to exercise the rescued animals. So, while we were there, we pitched in and had a pleasant afternoon. As we were leaving, a rather large Pointer attached himself to me. He literally wrapped his long legs around me and wasn't letting go.

That was it.

I had no intention of having a dog, let alone rescuing one. But I couldn't bear the thought of leaving him behind. He had a skin disease and, until it was proven not to be contagious, he was chained up in isolation.

Skin disease or not, he was the most beautiful dog I'd ever seen.

Sure enough, less than a month later, he was home with us, welcomed with open arms and hearts. I named him Walter (it suited him somehow) and he fitted in as though we'd always had him. He was the best dog ever. Although he was big, he was incredibly chilled out and never barked. In fact, he took being chilled out to a whole new level – but that made him especially endearing.

True to form, that evening, as we were choosing a film, Walter was asleep.

Suddenly and very out of character, both dogs jumped up from their sleep and ran, barking loudly, towards the closed lounge door. The barks turned to growls, which didn't stop. It surprised us all and I was unnerved but I instinctively got up, thinking I'd open the door so they could get to whatever it was they were barking and growling at.

With their noses at the door, I couldn't get it open. I asked them to move back but neither one of them would budge.

I gently nudged them both backwards until I could prise the door open. I expected them to dash out at whatever was causing their distress but surprisingly – and increasingly scarily – they still refused to move. I gently tried to encourage them forward, to no avail.

I couldn't see any danger out there, so I went into the hall myself and called them to come to me. Still, they wouldn't move.

They were still growling, fur standing up at the back of their necks. I thought that only happened in cartoons, but I discovered that evening that it was true – and a little unnerving.

Baring their teeth and continuing to growl, they both started walking backwards, very slowly, into the middle of the lounge.

I felt chills run up and down my spine.

I went back into the lounge and called them. Finally, they turned around, came to me and everything went back to normal.

Except it wasn't normal.

I was thankful that I wasn't alone. We talked about it for the next few minutes and comforted the dogs. The only rational explanation was that perhaps a cat was outside, and they had got scent of it.

We put the film on. I watched it for a few minutes before leaving the room. I was on a mission. I didn't say a thing to Aaron or Rob, but I intended to take photos and I didn't want to scare them or make them ruminate on what had happened. After all, it isn't every day that the dogs would refuse to enter the hall. In fact, it had never happened before. There had to be a reason, right?

There had been activity in the hall several times – and I have photographic evidence of some of that. What the dogs had done piqued my interest.

We'd usually take photos in the hall, but tonight I chose to go upstairs to the landing. Little did I know that I would capture something quite significant and difficult to disprove but again, I'll let you be the judge of that.

As I snapped away, I didn't see a thing, but I remember being very nervous. It was pitch black, with no light from the moon to illuminate my way. I was scared that I'd see something, so I was talking to myself to mentally prepare myself in case I did.

I walked down the stairs to the half landing and took more photos. This time, I saw orbs as the photos were being taken. There were lots of them and, I must admit, I was getting rather blasé about them. I wasn't surprised to have captured something, given the extreme and rare behaviour of the dogs.

The multiple orbs didn't bother me at all. But what was revealed when I reviewed the pictures certainly did.

I'd been brave for long enough. The feeling of fear was intensifying, so I called it quits and looked at the photos I'd taken.

Part of me wished I hadn't.

I was spooked to see a small blob on the left of the photo. It was a dark lilac that's difficult to describe – and certainly not anything like I'd seen before. All the previous images had been either white or on the blue spectrum. I dragged the photo to enlarge that area and got the shock of my life. Again though, I'll leave it to your judgement.

I took a few minutes to compose myself and went back into the lounge. I didn't want to frighten the two of them by blurting out what I'd just experienced but it was difficult to contain my feelings.

I couldn't focus on watching the film with them. It was a blur. It probably appeared as though I was paying attention, but my thoughts were firmly focused on what had happened with the dogs, and then the photographic evidence.

I didn't show them the image until the next day. They were as surprised as I was and said they were glad I hadn't shared it with them the previous evening.

Chapter 24

As I've already mentioned, West Grove is a sizable house. Sitting within its own gardens, it hasn't any close neighbours and can be a little creepy on dark winter evenings. As well as that, the walls are so thick, it's difficult to hear any noise from room to room. It would be very easy for someone to wander around the house without being heard.

That's partly why we installed such a sophisticated alarm system. It was reassuring to know that we could use the intercom to speak to someone in a control room if we ever needed to. If the alarm was triggered, all we had to do was provide our password to confirm we were OK – and take a good look around, to make sure all was well, of course. If the control room didn't hear from us, the procedure was that they'd call the police. As I am sure you can imagine, we felt comforted by the presence of this system. That is…until we didn't…

"What on earth?"

I awoke in a state of shock and confusion. Was that our house alarm? A few muddled seconds passed before Martin and I were able to think straight and realise that the noisy siren, blaring relentlessly, was indeed our alarm.

I turned the bedside light on.

We looked at each other without saying a word and sprang into action. Well, Martin did. I leapt out of bed, whispering, "What do we do next?"

The bedroom door was closed (that's another story – I'll explain later), so we were able to whisper to each other. It's hard to understand the thoughts that might run through your mind until you find yourself in such a position.

Initially, I was optimistic that it was a false alarm. We didn't have anything to fear, and all would be well shortly. But then, my thoughts went full circle. There must be a reason for the alarm to go off – and that reason was most likely that someone had entered the house. Should we leave the bedroom and risk encountering them?

The dilemma was solved in that instant. Martin opened the bedroom door and ventured out onto the landing. He crossed the landing and turned the light on, calling out in a loud, booming tone. I think he intended to intimidate, and it worked for me!

After a few seconds, he walked slowly but surely, step by stealthy step, down the stairs.

I followed, in the same manner. It was like a scene from Laurel and Hardy.

As we got to the hall, we heard the voice from the alarm system, asking for the password. We gave it and had a brief chat with the controller, confirming that we'd have a look round the perimeter of the property (which took a few minutes) before reporting back.

Thankfully, everything appeared to be fine. All the windows and doors were checked and there wasn't anyone to be seen.

We went back to bed and before long, we were both fast asleep. All's well that ends well.

Until the next time. And there was a next time. And a next time and another next time and…well, I guess you get the gist.

This escapade – alarm sounding in the middle of the night, nothing to be seen – became a regular occurrence. Our patience eventually ran out, we called the alarm company and insisted that an engineer come and see what the problem was. We were thankful that they were false alarms, but nonetheless it was becoming annoying. This was a paid-for service after all.

A couple of days later, a rather pleasant chap arrived and conducted a very thorough investigation. You've guessed it: he couldn't find anything wrong.

He couldn't offer any explanation, so I asked what we should do next? We didn't appreciate being regularly woken in the middle of the night. Apologies were forthcoming and he reassured us that the system was working.

"Don't hesitate to get in touch again, if this continues," he called, as he left.

"I will," I replied. And I thought to myself, *Don't you worry about that*!

Two weeks later, he was back. Very friendly, very thorough, and very apologetic again. But, just as the first time, he couldn't find any fault in the system and couldn't offer any explanation.

Brilliant (not).

I'll fast forward to the fifth visit. Feeling this part of the story is a bit monotonous? Imagine how we felt! Especially as there didn't appear to be a solution to the ongoing problem.

This time, he gave me a detailed explanation of how the system operated, told me what was needed for the alarm to function correctly and walked me, step by step, through the whole check.

The monitor for the system was in the hall, and had to be plugged in at all times. A probe displayed the level of energy flowing through the system. The level kept fluctuating, and this, he thought, must be the problem. It needed to be above 50 megahertz and, while this would be displayed, it would then drop somewhere below 20 megahertz, within seconds.

This didn't mean that much to me, but the engineer assured me that it was highly unusual. In fact, he'd never experienced this phenomenon and that's why he couldn't offer any explanation.

But then he did.

He asked, albeit in a light-hearted manner, "You haven't got a ghost, have you?"

"Ha, ha, ha, ha! Very amusing," I said. But I was thinking, "Oh no, funny you should mention that…"

I must be honest. The paranormal activity being to blame had crossed my mind, but I didn't want to give any credence to it.

So, there it is.

Things continued in this manner for several more weeks. Eventually, we reluctantly decided that enough was enough and cancelled the contract with the alarm company, going forward without an alarm.

We really had no choice if we wanted uninterrupted sleep. A fault couldn't be found, so there was no way to fix it.

The mystery of the alarm being triggered for no apparent reason was never solved.

Chapter 25

I mentioned that our bedroom door was closed. Well, here's the explanation.

For many years, we would always sleep with it open.

There were two main reasons for this. First, we wanted to be able to hear if anything untoward happened during the night – particularly before we had the alarm installed. Second, we wanted to listen out for our daughter, because the sheer size of the property meant we felt she was quite a distance from us.

After the night when her friend stayed over and they woke up believing they'd seen a ghost, our vigilance was heightened. After all, Aaron was so frightened and upset, she couldn't bring herself to sleep in her room for six weeks afterwards.

I didn't know until sometime after, but Martin often used to wake with a feeling that he was being watched – as though someone was standing outside the bedroom door, looking in. He'd also get a frequent sensation that he'd almost caught a glimpse of someone walking past the bedroom doorway.

He kept it to himself for quite a while, not wanting to frighten me and doubting whether he was seeing anything at all. But he eventually admitted it and confessed that it regularly scared him.

The fact that he chose to keep quiet resonated with me. I did the same, for all manner of things…feeling someone beside me on the bed or my pillow, seeing white misty shapes, seeing orbs, and so on.

Waking in the night and catching a glimpse of a perceived presence on the landing eventually happened so often that Martin reluctantly decided that if he wanted a full night's sleep, he'd have to close the bedroom door. We comforted ourselves with the thought that the newly-installed alarm would make up for this – at least until the 'alarming' (couldn't help that!) situation of its continued unexplained triggering led us to turn it off.

Closing the door solved Martin's interrupted nights, but it led to a further creepy situation.

When we woke up in the morning, we'd regularly find our bedroom door open. There was no rational explanation as to how or why. It didn't swing open at any other time and besides, the bottom of the door caught slightly on the carpet, requiring some pressure for it to open, so it didn't seem feasible that it would open of its own accord. Plus that carpet meant it didn't open silently.

It became something we just lived with. It was a bit unsettling but, over time, we accepted it as the norm, and put it to the back of our minds.

The only time it came to the fore for me was when I was alone in the house, but on these rare occasions, tiredness always prevailed, and I slept safely and soundly, regardless of the door mystery. Besides, it appears that whoever was lurking on the landing, often made their way to the bed, either on my pillow or lying behind me.

Chapter 26

Over the years that followed, I became particularly close to my sister-in-law, Andrea. Although she lived more than 40 miles away, she'd come to visit, or I'd stay over with her and my brother regularly.

As our relationship deepened, she began to come over more often. I was pleased to have her company and I was glad she was completely unfazed by the stories that had been told over the years. She was a complete and utter cynic about anything remotely related to the paranormal.

It wasn't necessarily that she didn't believe me. But she knew that until she experienced something for herself, she wasn't going to accept the existence of anything she couldn't see. She'd respond to anything I said on the subject with humour, finding it all hilarious.

But that was about to change.

The more frequently Andrea visited, the more likely she was to experience something for herself. I secretly wanted her to share the fright and wonder – and I wasn't to be disappointed.

Unlike Andrea, I have a couple of friends who would happily visit me at West Grove, but were adamant that they wouldn't stay over, such was their fear of the unknown. Even though I'd shared very little of my experiences with them, that was clearly enough for them to want to take their leave before dark!

One evening, Andrea was at West Grove and we'd chosen a movie to watch. Unfortunately, it was a bit boring, so we were racking our brains for something to do.

She was feeling mischievous and adventurous – and not in the least nervous. Why should she be? She hadn't experienced anything untoward. She'd seen my photos though and, ever the cynic, she suggested it would be 'fun' to turn the lights off and call out to the room.

I wasn't so sure. Let's face it, this was nothing new to me, and while I lived with the various experiences as they arose, I was never responsible for asking for things to happen – they just did. It wasn't necessarily something that I'd encourage.

Still, she appeared amused by the thought of having a 'call out' and I'd never felt or seen anything sinister, so why not amuse her?

I was uneasy, but faced with her cynicism and a desire to have fun, I agreed that we'd make a light-hearted attempt at seeing if there was anybody there. It would be just like in the movies.

We agreed that we'd take flash photos. I don't mind admitting that I was a little anxious. After all, although she was staying the night, she would soon be going home and leaving it all behind. I had to continue here, and if anything unsettling occurred, it would be me that would have to live with it.

That's why I refused to video anything, which would have recorded audio, as well as images. I was adamant that it was a step too far. What if something was captured on video and that something had dark intent? No thanks. I had enough to tolerate without escalating things further.

"Let's go in the garden," I suggested. "I've never captured anything outside and it's winter, so there are good conditions for capturing light anomalies."

Off we went and Andrea started taking photos randomly. The garden lit up every time with the flash of the camera, but we didn't capture anything. After five minutes, I started to sense where to direct the camera. I can't explain how or why but it was a very subtle feeling.

"There!" I would say, and Andrea would point the camera in the right direction.

"There!" I'd say again, and we continued in this way for the next few minutes.

"Woah! What was that?"

I'd seen what looked like a long line of what I can best describe as cloudy, white mist. Andrea said she'd seen the same. Well, she'd seen something, at least.

"Let's have a look at the photos."

We ran through the images, and sure enough, captured in several of the photos were light anomalies. They appeared as cloudy, white, misty, cylindrical shapes and in one or two of the photos, these were many feet in length, extending from the bottom of the frame to the top.

"Wow! I told you!"

It's interesting – and I can't explain it – that sometimes anomalies are captured in a photo when you haven't seen anything with the naked eye, and sometimes the opposite is true. And sometimes it's the flash lighting that means you're able to see something. When that happens, I don't mind admitting that it makes me jump. No matter how much I try to prepare myself, it's still a surprise that shocks me into a gasp or a feeling of apprehension – and I can never predict which.

"Let's move around to the side of the house," I suggested. We strolled a short distance and stood close to the well, near the high stone wall that separates the front and back gardens.

Again, I started directing Andrea where to point the camera and, sure enough, we spotted more light anomalies, varying in brightness and length. I'd asked her to face the gate in the wall, which had been the entrance into the grounds for so many locals visiting the doctor's surgery many years ago. My rationale was that we were perhaps seeing residual energy.

The light anomalies we'd caught on camera hadn't been enough to shift Andrea's scepticism. She still hadn't vocalised any acceptance of the paranormal. But what was to happen next totally transformed her, in an instant.

Her scepticism was her prerogative. Although when I challenged her, she couldn't deny that something was happening, despite being unable to offer a logical explanation.

We were standing near the well, chatting about the fact that I had read somewhere that water, particularly slow-moving or stagnant water, may be a conduit for spiritual energy. It was something I'd heard on my journey to search for rational explanations for the various experiences I'd had over the years. I thought it was worth a mention, particularly because it was part of my logic for moving toward the well.

As I was explaining this, we stood almost shoulder to shoulder, with my sister-in-law to my right, both of us facing the gate. She had her hands raised, holding the phone camera, and I began to suggest where she should focus next.

Out of nowhere there appeared a large, shimmering, bright gold, perfectly spherical object, about the size of a small football, that hovered about an inch from her face to the right of her head.

It wasn't translucent; it was solid and a beautiful silky gold colour. I can't repeat the swear words hurtling through my head. I was completely taken aback and incredibly excited, all at the same time.

As I was attempting to gather my thoughts and express them, she blurted out, "What the hell is that?"

It was still there, hovering in a shimmering sort of way (my best description again, sorry!). As she spoke, we both turned our heads to face the object, as opposed to seeing it peripherally. It hovered for a second or two longer, and then shot off out of sight so quickly, we could barely see it leave.

We stood staring at each other with startled expressions for what felt like forever but was probably only a moment or two. I left it to Andrea to speak.

"I can't believe I've just seen that," she said.

"What did you see?" I wanted her to describe it so that she would corroborate my experience without me leading her in any way.

"A large, gold ball hovering next to my head that just shot off when we turned to look at it."

"Yep. Exactly."

"I can't believe it," she said again.

My reply was a long time coming.

"Now you know how I feel. I can't believe it either, but I'm so glad that you've seen this. Welcome to my world."

"Oh my god – I've just seen a gold ball," she continued. "It was real, but what the hell was it?"

It may have been a rhetorical question, but I knew exactly how she felt. I'd had so many similar experiences, her feeling of excitement and overwhelming surprise resonated with me. It was that feeling of knowing it was real but being unable to say what it was and why it was there.

That finished our session – on a high note – and we ventured back inside.

You can imagine what we talked about for the next hour or so. She called home and told my brother – and I know that feeling too; the compulsion to share the experience with someone, if only to stop yourself going mad with your thoughts.

I now had an ally, which was a very pleasant feeling.

Chapter 27

By now, it was the norm for me to take photos. I was mostly home alone and experiencing these events with no-one else around to share them with.

I'd spent years questioning myself about what was happening and whether I was imagining or seeing things. Weeks would pass with nothing happening – and that begged the question, was I imagining it? Or had the anomalies left, seeking refuge elsewhere? But then – boom – it would start again.

What better way, then, to reassure myself that I wasn't going crazy than to gather – or at least attempt to gather – photo evidence? It worked for me on several levels and there was often something to be seen.

One evening varied from the usual. I still captured anomalies but in a way that I hadn't experienced before.

I'd intentionally kept these experiences from Brad, the young man I was fostering. Firstly, for the obvious reason that I didn't want to scare him. After all, he had to live here, and he would sometimes be home alone. And secondly, I didn't want to influence him one way or the other in the world of the paranormal – or the 'absolutely normal', as I now call these experiences.

I was taking flash photos in the lounge, and, after a few minutes, I felt drawn to the hall and ventured out there. I took several photos and, sure enough, anomalies appeared.

So far so good. I'd somehow become so blasé that this was nothing exceptional. But as the next photo flash went off, I caught a huge apparition that set my heart racing.

It was Brad!

"Don't do that! You scared me!" he exclaimed.

"I scared you? You scared me!" I replied, knowing we could go around in circles here.

"What are you doing?" he asked.

Fair question. But how could I answer it without giving the game away?

"I'm just taking photos," I said.

"What of? Ghosts?"

And there was me thinking I'd kept all this on the downlow.

I pondered for a moment and then recalled that, of course, I'd shown him the photo I'd taken when I had the overwhelming feeling of love.

What to do next? I wanted to continue with the photos, but the game was up.

"Can I have a go?" asked Brad.

"Are you sure you want to?"

He wanted to, so we began.

"If there is anybody here, make your presence known. Come towards us." Yep, it was a bit clichéd but there you go; that's what we said.

The camera flashed, the hall was lit up, and there wasn't anything to get excited about. We carried on for several minutes in this manner, and Brad was a tad disappointed with his first attempt.

"You'll need to be patient," I explained. "I'm sure ghosts don't necessarily appear to order."

Little did I know, but, as they say, ignorance is bliss.

"I know," he said. "Carry on."

We did and, as I've regularly captured anomalies on the stairs that appear to move upwards (well, that's where the orbs are in sequential photos), I suggested that he took pictures as I walked up the stairs.

"Right", I said, "Are you ready?"

I stood at the bottom of the stairs and called out, "If you're here, please walk up the stairs with me."

I walked slowly up the stairs while Brad took photos, the camera flashing away. Halfway up, I turned around and made my way slowly down, Brad still snapping away. We hadn't captured anything untoward.

As I went from the bottom step to the hall floor, the flash lit up the hall and there it was – exactly what we'd been waiting for.

Even though I'd been calling out to entice the presence, a large part of me didn't truly think anything would appear. What a fool! I jumped out of my skin.

"Woah!" exclaimed Brad. "What was that?"

I didn't answer but Brad was very excited and animated and kept on repeating, "I saw that, I saw that!"

"I know! I did too."

"What did you see?"

"I think I've got it on camera."

There was a picture of me jumping up in the air with my arms up in excitement at seeing something with my own eyes as the flash went off. Believe me, something materialising in front of your eyes makes you feel excited and anxious all rolled into one.

Beside me, at almost head height, was a large white orb. It was cylindrical, and somewhat blurry, as though captured while moving. It appeared in the photo to be approximately a foot long and had its own luminosity. How could that be? I've never been able to find an answer. Incidentally, I'm a bit blurred in the image too, having been captured mid-jump.

So, what do we do next? Perhaps unsurprisingly, we continued taking photos.

Drat and double drat, there wasn't a thing to get excited about thereafter. We continued. Time was on our side, and I assume it was also on the side of anything that was present – they may have been hanging around this old building for some considerable time.

Frame after frame, we didn't capture anything further but then… There was a flash, but the image was completely dark. It was as if there hadn't been a flash at all.

Strange.

Flash! Again, the picture was completely dark. This continued for the next 18 photos.

Click, flash, darkness.

It felt increasingly strange. The camera was working but not in the usual manner. I couldn't figure this out. I had an idea though. Without saying a word to Brad, I walked into the lounge and took a couple of photos.

"What are you doing?" he asked.

"You'll see."

Click, flash, a completely normal photo.

Click, flash, completely normal photo.

I walked back into the hall.

Click, flash, darkness. I kid you not.

Although going into the lounge had proved the camera wasn't broken, I wasn't necessarily any the wiser. I couldn't figure out how this could be.

I've kept the sequence of photos and for good reason. You see, this wasn't as straightforward as it appeared. Of course, the fact that the flash went off, but the picture was in complete darkness was strange enough – but it was to become even stranger.

"Shall we call it a day?" Brad had seen enough and was still excited about what we'd captured on the photo and seen with our eyes – an especially powerful validation for him.

He took himself off up to his room and I settled down to watch TV in the lounge. Except, as usual, I didn't. As usual, I ran through the photos we'd taken, still on a high from the evidence captured and us both experiencing the same thing.

It might seem strange to review a sequence of photos that don't appear to contain anything. But by then, I was becoming experienced, and I knew there could be a tiny speck of something worth further perusal.

I wasn't disappointed.

On the third frame, there appeared to be a mist-like shape to the left of the picture. It stood out against the background of the hall wall, which is painted a very dark grey. The shape appears to be approximately three feet in length and six inches wide.

It was difficult to determine but I zoomed in on this 'mist'. I realised it was pale blue/grey and denser towards the centre. I dragged the photo more, to enlarge the image further and studied it in shock.

There was a face. It was clearly a male face, with the eyes, nose, mouth, and moustache easily distinguishable now that the area was enlarged.

I sat and pondered it for a minute or so, feeling rather spooked but also amazed at what had been captured. As mentioned, I still have the sequence of photos, including this one. But time moved on, as always, and I was busy and didn't dwell on the evening for any length of time.

I admit though, I particularly enjoyed this experience, because it was shared. That always reassured me in a variety of ways, not least that I wasn't going mad.

On more than one occasion, I overheard Brad telling his friends that he'd seen and captured images of orbs. After that, one or two of his friends would visit solely for the purpose of discussing the goings-on and the subject in general. They seemed genuinely curious and fascinated in equal measure.

Chapter 28

I like to keep fit. There's a history of heart disease on my father's side of the family and that's enough reason to care for myself, having suffered his sudden death of a heart attack when he was only 45 and I'd just, that day, turned 18.

My grandfather also dropped dead of a heart attack in the street, after visiting us, when he was in his 60s. My grandmother suffered from angina for most of her life, too, so I take care of my heart health.

In all honesty, it comes easy for me. I enjoy eating healthily and being active. I was only four years old when I started ballet and tap lessons, moving on through dance performances, fencing for my high school and county, as well as horse riding and, of course, boxing training. 'Take your pick' is my approach to keeping fit. Whatever I enjoy is good enough for me. Otherwise, who would bother?

I like to work out when I can, but I particularly enjoy swimming. It's my form of meditation, clocking up the lengths at a leisurely pace, without a care in the world. I usually go in the evening when the pool is quieter, and mentally drift away.

A new leisure facility had recently opened near our home. Millions of pounds had been invested in the refurbishment, including an Olympic-sized pool. Wow! Let's go! I persuaded my middle daughter, Lydia, to join with me, and we were excited to get started.

Anyone who's been a gym member will be aware that you must do an induction. I didn't necessarily need one – I was by then a fully-qualified personal trainer and England ABAE boxing coach – but as each facility has different equipment, I always think it's useful to go along and learn about what's on offer. It shortcuts the learning curve.

Lydia and I were excited about training together and we went along to our induction evening, armed with our swimming gear, in case we decided on a dip afterwards. That meant we had to find a locker and here's where it could have got complicated. We discovered that they weren't free to use. We needed a pound coin or a locker token. We had neither.

Going home wasn't an option – we hadn't even got started yet.

I walked up to the bank of doors, saying how nice everywhere looked and that no expense had been spared, not only on the style and quality of the lockers but on the number of them too. There were hundreds.

With that, I randomly opened one door among the vast array and put our belongings inside, hoping that we could visit reception and borrow a token.

But we didn't need to. Unbelievably, I discovered that the person who had previously used the locker must have left their token behind. There it was, sitting in the well of the coin slot, waiting to be picked up.

"We can use this!" I called to my daughter.

As I picked it up, I noticed that it wasn't the standard token. I don't have an extensive knowledge of locker tokens, but I assumed it was unusual because it was pink, with an engraving on it.

As I looked at it, I saw something that might not seem profound to anyone reading this, but which certainly felt that way to me. The token was engraved with white angel's wings and the words 'Daddy's Girl' written just below them.

I paused for a moment. I was a Daddy's girl. All my life, those words had been used to describe me by friends and relatives because I was inseparable from my dad.

We used the token, completed our Induction and training session, and returned to gather our things. I couldn't leave it behind and popped it in my purse.

After that, I always carried it with me. Every time I used it, it reminded me of the strange coincidence. And it also made me question the whole concept of coincidence. Perhaps everything happens for a reason?

I truly believe now that there's no such a thing as coincidence. I admit that I don't always know what the reason is for any event or occasion, but I believe there is one.

Several months later, I discovered I couldn't locate the token. I couldn't believe that I'd mislaid it – and I was upset. I always carried it around in my purse and used it regularly. But it was gone.

I called Lydia and explained how upset and annoyed I was with myself. How could I possibly have lost it? The thought of leaving something so cherished in a supermarket trolley seemed highly improbable.

Nonetheless, it was gone. Bizarre as it seems to be so upset over a token, I felt sad. I knew there would be an explanation – it just escaped us for the time being.

The answer came several days later.

It was a beautiful sunny day, and I'd washed all the bedding and hung it out to dry. I was feeling especially pleased with myself and, as I was on the last wash load, I was looking forward to relaxing with a cup of coffee. I shook out the last fitted sheet and pegged it out.

Picking up the wash basket and walking back inside, I put the kettle on. I turned back to the basket to take it upstairs while the kettle was boiling, and lo and behold, there, in the middle of the lid, was the token.

I was delighted – but couldn't fathom it.

I called Lydia again and explained the sequence of events. She couldn't believe it either.

I truly couldn't figure this out. If the token was in the washing, which it must have been, why didn't it fall out in the machine? If it had survived falling out in the machine, how did it not fall out of the washing when it was being hung on the line? And if it was in the washing, how did it end up on the lid of the basket, after I'd carried it in from the garden? Surely, I'd have noticed it? And surely it would have fallen off while I was carrying it?

All these questions, and no answers, Story of my life!

Chapter 29

I hope you'll understand why I dwelled on the mystery around the returning token for quite a while – and that wasn't to be the end of the bizarre events.

I'm a prolific reader and have been from a young age. I've read my favourite authors' books several times over, and I'm happy to read fiction and non-fiction – I particularly like crime thrillers.

It was July, my birthday month, and I was enjoying a crime thriller by an author who was new to me. It was a page-turner if ever there was one. I liked his style of writing and because I've read most books by my favourite authors, it's great to find someone new to enjoy.

I must confess, I'm often not aware of the titles of books. I prefer to select by author, or the blurb on the back cover. And that's how I chose this book.

My birthday is always a poignant time for me. The memories of my dad passing away when I turned 18 return every year. A happy day that's forever tinged with sadness.

The last time I saw my dad, he was in hospital. I held his hand. I talked and he listened because he could only speak with difficulty. I broke down in tears until, after several hours,

I was led away by a nurse, who advised me to go home. Reluctantly, I left.

The call to rush back to the hospital came several hours later. I didn't go back. I couldn't bear to do so. Mum did and I've never regretted my decision. Mum arrived home with two of our best family friends, and I knew. They didn't need to speak. Life changed, and it was a devastating time.

As usual, on my birthday I was thinking of Dad. I talked to him – I'm certainly not the only person who does that, when a loved one has passed on. It works for me.

I asked for a sign so that I knew he was listening and present, although I felt as though I was asking too much. Part of me believed I was talking to myself, although I wasn't especially concerned about that – somehow, there was comfort in simply speaking out loud to him. But it would make for an extra special birthday if I could experience something tangible. After all, I'd seen the big, white feather in my living room, so it wouldn't be the first time I'd received a sign, although admittedly, I hadn't asked for it that time.

The day was enjoyable. I had the usual birthday greetings, gifts, and a celebration meal with my family. There were no signs, although I wasn't necessarily disappointed. I didn't really expect to receive one; it was just wishful thinking. I was comforted just to have Dad in my thoughts.

At bedtime, I noticed something on the floor. About a foot away from the pillow end of my bed, lay a large white feather.

Wow! How did that get there? I turned around and checked. There weren't any windows open and anyway, the house is three storeys high – I'd never previously seen a feather float in randomly.

It's common knowledge that spirits who want their presence known will send white feathers to loved ones. I saw it as a sign, I was excited and incredibly thankful. I talked again to Dad and thanked him for finding the energy to answer my call. I was so happy. What a way to end the day!

But it didn't end there.

I usually read in bed to wind down and rest my mind. In fact, I often fall asleep holding onto my book. This evening, after seeing the feather, I was a little distracted. Joyful, but distracted. I had to re-read some of the pages several times, as I couldn't focus on what I was reading. Eventually, I became consumed by the story and managed to absorb the content.

As I came to the end of a chapter, I was so impressed with the way the book flowed that I thought I should make a note of the author, intent on reading his other books.

Turning to the front cover, to check out his name, the title suddenly leaped out at me. 'Daddy's Girl'. No way! Another sign! I was so excited I truly couldn't focus on the book, again. I'd had no idea that this was the title – but what a coincidence.

Except it wasn't. As I say, I believe there are no coincidences.

What a birthday it had turned out to be. With that, I turned off the light and snuggled down to sleep.

You've guessed it, I was so excited, I struggled, at first, to nod off.

Eventually, I felt drowsy and was drifting off, too tired to think or keep my eyelids open any longer.

Suddenly, a voice said, "Anne."

It was loud and clear, inside my head. And it was my dad's voice.

This is truly exactly what I experienced. Of course, I would know my dad's voice. I accept that it may be difficult to believe, but I can only state my reality.

My eyelids sprang open, and I leapt out of bed. After the surprise, excitement overcame me. Tears sprung forth as I paced about the bedroom, thanking Dad profusely.

Can you imagine the feeling? It's difficult to explain but the words were spoken inside my head. I didn't hear them audibly – that's the only way I can describe it.

What a day!

Eventually, I fell asleep, with a smile on my face. It was the best birthday ever.

If you're curious, no, I haven't heard Dad again since. It's been more than 10 years. I hold onto the memory of this very special day and will cherish it always.

There was to be another occasion when I captured something that I'd called out for on a very recent birthday, but that's for later.

Chapter 30

It was a night like many others; mundane and minus the distraction of orbs (hooray!).

The evening was a most welcome relief from the usual distraction of anomalies floating around the room. The full-on demands of running the business, combined with our coaching roles, meant we had a lot of responsibilities and demands on our time. So, outside that, our life was simple. We wanted to spend the odd evening in front of the TV, to unwind from the usual rigour and stresses of the day.

Fat chance! For me, at least. But this evening was as peaceful as I could hope for. Finally, it was time for bed, and I fell asleep rapidly, after a long and tiring day.

I woke up suddenly in the middle of the night. What on earth was going on?

I was lucid enough that questions were hurtling into my semi-conscious state at a rapid rate. I lay still, frozen in shock. I was experiencing something new and bizarre. I could feel it – as opposed to the usual visual sensations – but I still questioned what I was experiencing.

I'm not sure I've ever figured it out. My whole body, head to toe, was vibrating. It's an inept description but I'm somewhat at a loss for the appropriate words. I appreciate that it's a very loose explanation, but I was experiencing a buzzing sensation, like an electric shock without any of the pain or discomfort associated with it.

If you're wondering how I can describe an electric shock, I'll take you back to the days when I had a pony. I frequented the farm daily, in all weathers – and often in the rain.

When we turned the horses out into the field, or when we rode out during the winter months, we had to go through a gate. The gate was metal, the gate posts were wooden, with a very heavy metal chain that hooked over and held the gate closed. The field was protected by an electric fence and in heavy rain, the water would soak the gate post and conduct electricity from the fence into the metal chain.

We'd often forget that it had rained and would, unthinkingly, grab the chain to open the gate. Yikes!

Too late, we'd be reminded by a shot of electricity, strong enough to jolt you out of your reverie, but not enough to impart any long-lasting damage. The pain was short-lived but (pardon the pun) shocking. We would snatch our hands away, but the sensation would last a few seconds more. It's very similar to touching something extremely hot and snapping your hand back when you feel the burn.

It caused a buzzing sensation, as the electricity was conducted from the metal. I'd feel it throughout my body, particularly strongly in my hand and arm.

If we remembered what was to come when the weather conditions were ripe, we'd simply pick up a stick and use it to lift the chain carefully over the gate post and enter the field without any unnecessary suffering! We were young and rather foolish and infinitely forgetful, so this happened a lot in the winter months. We found it quite comical, to be honest, when it happened to someone else and not yourself.

Back to this night and the strange buzzing sensation. I didn't have a clue what was happening, but I was aware of it. I lay still for what seemed like an age but was most likely only a minute at the most. The feeling didn't reduce or stop.

Suddenly, completely unexpectedly and without explanation, I heard voices. They were talking rapidly, inside my head, not audibly through my ears. Again, the description feels inadequate but what else can I say? The sound was loud and in my head!

I could only lay and listen. I couldn't make sense of the words, but it was as clear and precise as though I was listening in on a telephone conversation between two strangers.

I became frightened – and then overwhelmed with fear. I'm not sure why; it was an irrational fear given that I was safely tucked up in bed and there wasn't anyone else in the room. But I wasn't in control of any of this, including the fact that it was happening in the first place.

Eventually, the voices ceased, the buzzing sensation faded away. It was over. But *what* was over? What was that exactly?

I had no idea. And still don't have any idea, even though this still happens randomly, albeit less frequently over the years.

I've tried to suppress my fear during these episodes, so that I can make sense of them but to no avail. Fear always wins out, and for a long time now, when I am woken up (or drifting to sleep) and the buzzing sensation starts, I silently repeat, in my head, the mantra, "Love and light, love and light, love and light, please protect me."

So far, this suffices – the buzzing sensation will usually recede rapidly without progressing to hearing the voices. I also say to myself, "Here we go again." I can't help it.

The first few times this happened, I didn't breathe a word to Martin. I was desperate to share the experience, but I suffered in silence. I didn't feel able to talk about it – it felt embarrassing to attempt to explain something that is quite unexplainable!

If the boot was on the other foot, so to speak, I'm not sure what I would have made of it. I'd most likely have dismissed it without much thought, as he did when I eventually told him. He probably thought I was going mad, but he didn't say so.

I wish I had an explanation about how or why this happens. Maybe one day I'll understand these episodes, but for now, my mantra will and does suffice.

Chapter 31

As I've mentioned, my sister-in-law, Andrea would often visit, sometimes with her grandchildren, who were then aged eight and 13. It was always fun.

We all enjoyed being outdoors when weather permitted – and sometimes even when it didn't. We have a log cabin in the garden, opposite the main house, and we had a TV and DVD player installed. Add a plush sofa, with too many furry throws to mention, as well as a log stove – and voila! The perfect retreat. Very cosy indeed.

One of our favourite evenings in the log cabin was around Christmas time, snuggling under the throws, watching a Christmas movie while watching the snow fall outside. I couldn't decide whether to sit back and gaze at the snow or watch the movie. I flitted between both. Bliss.

We finished off the perfect experience with mugs full of piping hot chocolate. We'd bought Christmas sweaters for the occasion, and we weren't disappointed by the weather or the movie – or our choice of sweaters!

During the summer months, we preferred to be outside (as much as is possible in the north). We'd go on trips out to the countryside or the coast or play outdoor games in the garden. One of our favourite pastimes was to spend the evening cooking outside, sitting around the log burner, with the cabin doors fully open, and music playing in the background.

The bats would come out at sunset, and we'd wait for them to make an appearance before going back into the house. There's something so very relaxing about being seated around a log fire when the evening is drawing in and the wildlife is beginning to stir.

The beautiful dog we had at the time, Walter the Third, would sit at our feet, enjoying the warmth and glow of the log fire. Even the cats would come and sit with us, no doubt waiting for any morsels of food left over from the evening meal. Yes, the two cats were a recent addition to the family.

We didn't always spend our evenings outside. When the weather was cooler, we'd retreat to the main house and have fun playing card and board games or watching a movie. Still very cosy, snuggled up on the sofas, covered with throws, with the log fire providing additional warmth and glow.

One winter's evening, it was, like many others, cold, wet and dark outside. The older child spoke up: "Have you seen any more ghosts lately Aunty Anne?"

I was surprised, because we'd never openly discussed anything relating to any of the experiences in their presence – or at least, at that point, I didn't remember having done so.

I asked her what she was referring to. She said she'd heard us talking on previous visits. So much for us keeping this whole topic on the downlow. Kids!

Andrea and I attempted to laugh it off and tried to distract her by changing the subject. After all, we were both conscious that the children slept over often, and whether justified or not, we were worried they might get scared, particularly at bedtime, if they had any inkling that 'ghosts' (her word not mine) might be roaming around.

The younger of the two was quite nervous about simply venturing to the toilet on his own after dark, even with the lights on!

But she wasn't falling for our changing the subject tactics.

"So, Aunty Anne, have you seen any ghosts recently?"

What should I say? The truth?

"How long have you got on that one?" I laughed – and feeling cowardly, I deferred to Andrea. "What do you think, Grandma?"

Andrea was equally stumped. She didn't have anything to say, and the silence was deafening. Incidentally, she would usually have a lot to say – and I hope she doesn't mind me saying so.

The granddaughter hadn't had an answer to her first question, so she tried a different tack.

"Have you taken any pictures recently?"

How did she know that too? Is she a mind reader? She wasn't. She'd simply overheard us, and we were so enraptured by our conversation we hadn't noticed that she was listening. I guess I would have found the subject interesting and well worth earwigging too, when I was her age.

I decided honesty was the best policy but first asked her to come into the kitchen with me, because I didn't want to respond honestly in the presence of her younger sibling.

"OK, yes, I have taken photos recently and yes, I have captured something and yes things are still happening. Happy now?"

"Do you do any call outs?"

"Call outs? Where have you got that from?"

"Oh, Mum watches lots of stuff on TV about ghosts and things."

"Ah. That's very different to experiencing things, you know."

"I know," she replied.

I was surprised that she didn't appear fazed by the subject or the thought that 'things went bump in the night' frequently here.

"Aunty Anne, can we do a call out?"

Wow. I didn't say anything. I wasn't sure how to respond. I was aware she wasn't my child, so it shouldn't be my decision. I worried how she would feel afterwards, regardless of whether anything happened or was captured. I wasn't sure how to go about doing a call out. What if we did and captured something dark? This is always a concern of mine, although I haven't experienced seeing anything dark-spirited.

And to be honest, I was thinking of myself, too. I had to live here when my guests had left, and if something was revealed that had been in abeyance, how would I deal with that?

I tended not to rock the boat and didn't call out anything specific. Everything that had happened had been incidental, without prompting, and a large part of my thought process was that I wanted it to remain that way.

But I was tempted. Would it be interesting? Would we get an intelligent response? Occasionally, I would still question whether anything tangible had happened at all, over the years.

During weeks without any activity, I'd question whether anything residual had dissipated, or anything visiting had departed. Or maybe it was my brain again and there was something physically wrong with me.

That said, thinking about everything that had happened, it was highly unlikely, particularly when other people had shared the experience. But I digress. Back to my niece. What should I do? What should I say?

"Give me a minute to think about it," I said, buying time.

"OK," she responded, and we ventured back into the lounge.

My sister-in-law was curious, as well she might be. I was too. The expression 'curiosity killed the cat' sprang to mind, but I parked the thought.

Curiosity won out.

"Let's do it!"

Andrea gave me a strange look, so while her grandson was distracted watching TV, I said I'd reveal all after the young man's bedtime.

He was due to go to bed in half an hour. Would I back out?

I wouldn't, and I didn't. Off he went to bed and a new phase of our experience began.

Chapter 32

Batten down the hatches and hang on – it's going to be a bumpy ride!

Before we got started, I sent up a silent prayer that it wouldn't be too bumpy. We didn't want to start with the clichéd, "Is there anybody there?" So, the three of us; me, my niece, and my sister-in-law, sat in the lounge and pondered on how we would do this.

I suggested we start where we were, and simply see if we got anything. We would talk to the room, taking photos at the same time and see what happened. I'd ruled out attempting to record, because I wasn't ready to hear anything like voices yet, given that Andrea and Demi would depart the following day, leaving me alone in the house. It was one thing to experience everything that had gone before, but another if something (or someone) were to speak – especially if it was negative. No way was I going to chance that, under any circumstances.

Nervous and inexperienced, we got the giggles. It took several minutes to contain ourselves and put on a straight face. Eventually, in very serious voices, we called out words to the effect of, "If you're here and watching us, make your presence known."

Silence reigned. Well, apart from the clicking of our phone cameras. I noticed I was holding my breath – as though that would make any difference! Oh, the anticipation!

My mind began to conjure up images and thoughts of what could happen next – and it wasn't anything to look forward to.

"Breathe Anne, breathe," I said to myself. "Relax."

I tried to. I wondered how the others were feeling but it wasn't the time to ask. You could hear a pin drop; such was the silence. Were they holding their breath too?

Silence, darkness, and more silence.

Things continued in this manner for 10 minutes or so and we didn't capture a thing. Phew! I felt a little ridiculous to be honest. I wasn't sure why I felt so anxious when I lived with this every day. But there you have it – I was.

We were sitting around the sides of the room, spread out on the sofas and I wasn't feeling anything untoward.

I broke the silence.

"Let's go into the hall. I often feel something in that area and let's face it, I've captured images there too."

Things were about to hot up (or become colder, depending on how you look at it).

The hall is relatively large and square, narrowing past the doorways to the dining room and lounge, with a small area offset at the far end, which consists of a playroom and downstairs loo. The staircase is approximately 10 feet from the door.

Initially, we were facing the stairway, standing in the centre of the hall. Again, we were talking to the room and clicking away on our phone cameras. But just as in the lounge, there wasn't anything to be seen. I began to relax, believing our actions were inconsequential. That turned out to be foolish.

We'd already said to each other that, in all honesty, if there was residual energy and that was causing these experiences, it will play out as and when, not when called upon to do so.

And if there was 'anyone' present, why would they perform for us? Why would they respond just because we wanted to be entertained? Would they even be aware of our presence?

Who knows? Not us, for sure – we could only assume. And we all know what happens when we assume. As the saying goes, it makes an 'ass' of 'u' and 'me'!

Even with all that in mind, we were prepared to sit it out for a while longer. I wasn't feeling it and my experience was that unless I was feeling it, it couldn't be forced. But that was to change – and rapidly, much to our delight and fright in equal measure.

I don't know why I thought of it at that specific moment, but I remembered the incident when our youngest daughter saw a ghost of a young girl in her room. I'd also noticed that the orbs often appeared to join the party, or at least make their presence known, when we were entertaining guests. Maybe some or any of the anomalies were of younger people – and perhaps they were drawn to other young people?

I asked my niece to sit in the middle of the floor in the hall and call out to anyone present, asking them to come and sit beside her. She did as I'd suggested, with a degree of trepidation. Who can blame her?

Bingo!

As she was speaking, we all saw a very bright, white light that lit up the hallway for a split second.

"Wow!" We all called out simultaneously.

Unbelievably, and incredibly bravely, my niece remained calm, despite being visibly excited. She called out again.

"Thank you for making your presence known. Please show us again that you're there."

We continued to click away with our cameras, even though we weren't experiencing anything visible to the naked eye.

After about five minutes of her sitting in the middle of the hall, while all three of us continued to call out, we glanced through the photos.

Lo and behold, the first photo exposed an unmistakable anomaly, immediately in front of my niece. It spanned somewhat wider than her frame, roughly level with her waist, approximately six inches in height.

It was so bright and luminous, it appeared to light up the whole area, particularly illuminating Demi. It was transparent – you could see my niece through it, although the surrounding space was in darkness, adding to the effect of the luminosity.

Contained within the glowing object was a rainbow of colour. And just for the record, it was pitch black outside, so there was no chance that it could be a reflection from the sun or the moon.

"I feel as though someone is behind me," Demi said. "I can sense someone there."

I suspected that she wasn't really feeling it, but the situation was making her imagination run riot. Easily done.

Even so, we took photos, and she was right. Behind, and slightly to the right of her, was a large, completely spherical, bright, white orb. On closer examination, we noticed there were two orbs present.

Wow (again).

"This is remarkable!" I don't mind admitting we were quite excited by all this.

Andrea sat down in the space vacated by my niece, we called out again and captured one photo with an orb present.

Then it was my turn. No sooner had I sat down than I caught sight of an orb close by

"I just saw something! Did you capture it?"

They had. It never ceases to amaze me when I see something and it's captured on a photo, proving that I wasn't imagining it.

After a while, we decided to call it quits in the hall and returned to the lounge. I put my arm around my niece's shoulder, asked her how she felt, and noticed that she was shaking.

She said she was scared (who wouldn't be?) but excited by what was going on. Although she was shaking, she didn't want to finish just yet. I asked her if she was sure, and she said she was.

I must stress that reading this narrative is far less anxiety-provoking than being there. There's no fear to be experienced by reading this narrative, but I can assure you it's a very different matter when you're immersed in the experience.

We did much of the same in the lounge, and again, captured much of the same. Eventually and reluctantly, we called it quits, as it was late, and we needed our sleep.

What an eventful and fulfilling evening! We were to repeat the experience in another productive session – more of that later. But I was mindful that, as successful and exciting as it was, I didn't want it to become a common occurrence. For one thing, it wasn't necessary – there wasn't anything to prove. But I also imagined it could easily become an unhealthy addiction.

That said, the excitement of the evening would eventually wear off, and the events became the usual faded memory.

Chapter 33

I was fast asleep, in a deep, deep sleep.

When suddenly, I wasn't!

I'd been awoken by the sound of loud knocking on the bedroom door. Well, I assumed it was knocking at the door. One minute I was fast asleep and then three loud knocks startled me awake.

"Yes?" I called out.

Silence.

"Yes?" I repeated, tersely. In my groggy state, my initial assumption was that one of the foster kids had knocked, needing me, but were, annoyingly, not responding.

Again, complete silence.

By now, I was sitting up in bed, feeling disorientated, and listening out for more sounds that didn't come. I sat in the dark, for what felt like an age and the silence remained.

I don't mind admitting that I was muttering to myself, in the dark, in the middle of the night.

Did I just imagine that or is someone out of bed? There weren't any lights on, and I couldn't hear anyone walking about. I don't think I imagined it – I'm wide awake. This was my reasoning.

The knocking sound was loud – almost as though it came from inside my head, while distinctly sounding like knocking on wood.

I was incredibly tired; my preference was to lay back down and go back to sleep. The pillow was incredibly inviting. Regrettably, my mind took charge and wouldn't let me rest. Curiosity got the better of me and I got out of bed, went to the door, and peered out into the darkness.

Thankfully, my eyes rapidly adjusted but there was nothing to experience except emptiness and stillness.

It crossed my mind that I should go downstairs and check for any strange activity, but my nervousness won out, so I didn't go any further than the bedroom door. Try it sometime – it's more nerve-wracking than it sounds, especially given everything that had gone before.

Hmm. Back to bed I went, muttering to myself. I knew I hadn't imagined the knocking. The loudness and the rapidity of my waking up was disturbing. Nevertheless, I was tired and, having sated my curiosity, I let my head hit the pillow and fell almost immediately into a deep sleep.

I woke up the next morning, relieved that I hadn't been disturbed again. Although I pondered the mysterious knocking for a few moments, I soon dismissed any worries and focused on getting on with the daily routine. I remember thinking, though, that this was a new one for me. I hadn't experienced anything like it before. Was there no end to the surprises in this home? I felt unsettled by the experience but didn't dwell on it.

It was a pleasant enough day, nothing untoward happened, thankfully. I thought about mentioning this new occurrence to my middle daughter, Lydia, when we spoke on the phone later that day, but it felt too insignificant. I was wrong. I chose not to pay any more attention to the knocking on the door. I couldn't think of a logical reason for it and left it at that.

Until it happened again.

About a week later I was again woken by the knocking. But this time, it sounded as though someone had rapped on the bedroom wall. There's a distinct difference between knocking on wood and knocking on plaster, and I noticed it, believe it or not.

So, here I was again, sitting up in bed, having been woken from a deep sleep by a loud knocking sound. Why?

This time, I didn't call out. I got out of bed immediately, to see if there was anyone else up. I'm not sure why, but I felt braver. Again, it was the middle of the night, pitch dark outside, and I was creeping about the landing.

Silence, darkness, and stillness.

I stood and listened, and let my eyes adjust to the lack of light.

It was a foolish thing to do. My mind started playing tricks on me, putting thoughts into my head.

"What if you see someone now, in front of you? If they just appear? What if someone knocks on the wall while you're standing here? What if there's another knocking sound and it comes from downstairs?"

I turned on the light and felt instant relief.

I had a look around downstairs, which I guess doesn't make any sense because the sound had been very close to me. Anyway, all was clear.

I went back to bed and this time it took a while to fall back to sleep. I now knew for sure that it wasn't my imagination.

But I still didn't have an answer for why I'd been woken in this way.

I focused on getting back to sleep, hoping that I wouldn't be disturbed again. My nervousness was unfounded though, and I woke naturally in the morning.

A few days later, Lydia called me again. This time I felt I had to share my strange experience with someone – and who better?

"I've got something to tell you", she said.

"I've something to tell you!" I replied. "You go first."

"I'm pregnant."

"Well, I didn't expect that! You're not kidding that you have news! That's wonderful. I'm so happy for you."

Lydia had been particularly close to my mum – her Nana Eileen. Mum passed when Lydia had turned 30. Although we'd often chat about how sad it was that Nana Eileen wouldn't be around to share the delight of further grandchildren, I wasn't aware that Lydia had any plans in that direction.

But I firmly believe Mum is around and looking out for us all and I knew she'd be especially pleased for Lydia when the time came for her children to make an appearance.

Lydia and her husband Scott had in fact, unknown to me, been trying for a baby for some time. We chatted about the baby news for a while before she remembered that I had news too. Of course, it paled into insignificance but as I'd mentioned it, she was curious to hear what I had to say.

I explained about both events. Lydia agreed that it was strange but didn't have an explanation either. She just accepted it and we went back to baby talk. She was clearly distracted with her pregnancy.

Everything went smoothly, and, in time, Lydia gave birth to a beautiful, healthy baby boy.

Time passed, and she'd talk about the next baby. They were hoping for a sibling to be close in age. How nice! I kept my fingers crossed for a brother or sister for her firstborn soon.

It was about two years before, suddenly, the knocking in the night started up again. It had been so long I'd almost forgotten about the previous instances. But again, the sound got my attention in much the same way.

The following day, I was immersed in my daily chores, when a thought suddenly struck me.

What if someone was trying to get my attention? But why would someone be trying to get my attention and who would that someone be?

I've no idea why that random thought popped into my head. I couldn't answer my own question, but I was inspired by my curiosity.

Lydia called and we chatted as usual and then, I asked, "Do you remember the knocking on the door and the wall that woke me out of my sleep?"

"Yes."

"It happened again – last night."

"You probably won't remember but it happened around the time you found out you were pregnant."

"Yes, I remember."

"Well…what if it was Mum trying to get my attention?"

There was a slight pause. Lydia probably disagreed with my rationale but didn't want to dishearten me. Oh well, I might as well share my thoughts fully. It came to me in a flash: if it's a sign, then I wanted to test it.

"Don't tell me if you're pregnant again, Lydia. Let me tell you."

There. I said it. She started to laugh, a nice kind of laugh. A laugh that seemed to say, "Yes Mum if that's what you believe, go ahead. Only time will tell."

"No, seriously, don't tell me, I want to tell you."

"OK Mum, you tell me when I'm pregnant."

I understood the note of cynicism in her voice. It was to be expected, But I knew – I just knew.

Over the years, I've come to know when certain things were to happen. I'd usually keep my own counsel on such things, but I was emboldened by events so I stuck my neck on the line on this one.

Some weeks later, you've guessed it, knock, knock, knock – I distinctly heard three knocks. My immediate thought was to call Lydia and put it to the test. So, I did. I was excited.

Lydia, though, replied that she wasn't. Wait, what? Oh, the disappointment! I admit I felt disappointed, and a little stupid if I'm honest, but hey ho, back to the drawing board.

I didn't have long to wait – a week to be precise, before Lydia called me.

She simply said, "I'm pregnant."

It transpires she was pregnant when I called but it was such early days, she couldn't have known.

So, there you have it. Now, on the rare occasion that I'm woken from my sleep by a sharp knocking sound, I wait in anticipation of news.

Epilogue

Finally, before I complete this narrative, I promised to tell you the conclusion to the strange occurrence of the one and only picture that came crashing down into the middle of the hall floor.

To refresh your memory, the picture was of four of our amateur boxers.

Several years on, one of the young boys in the picture had a horrific quad bike accident, which brought him close to death. It was a very arduous and lengthy journey back to good health for him, but I'm pleased to say that he has made a full recovery.

Was it a coincidence that this was the only one of our photos that he was in?

I'll let you decide. I know which side of the fence I sit on.

And that, as they say, is that.

Well, truth be known, there's likely to be more to come, but for now, I'll leave you in peace. I sincerely hope that whatever reason or journey has led you to my book, that you've enjoyed my True Story…